(100 YEARS OF POPULAR MUSIC)

The MILLENNIUM
edition

International Music Publications Limited

England: Griffin House
161 Hammersmith Road
London W6 8BS

Germany: Marstallstr. 8
D-80539 München

Denmark: Danmusik
Vognmagergade 7
DK1120 Copenhagen K

Carisch

Italy: Via Campania 12
20098 San Giuliano Milanese
Milano

Spain: Magallanes 25
28015 Madrid

France: 20 Rue de la Ville-l'Eveque
75008 Paris

Production: Sadie Cook, Ulf Klenfeldt and Miranda Steel

Published 1999

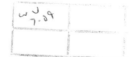

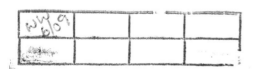

International Music Publications Limited
Griffin House 161 Hammersmith Road London W6 8BS England
Order Ref: 7139A

The MILLENNIUM edition

Contents
(a song for each year)

The MILLENNIUM *edition*

Contents
(in alphabetical order)

GOODBYE DOLLY GRAY

Words by WILL D COBB
Music by PAUL BARNES

Moderato marcato

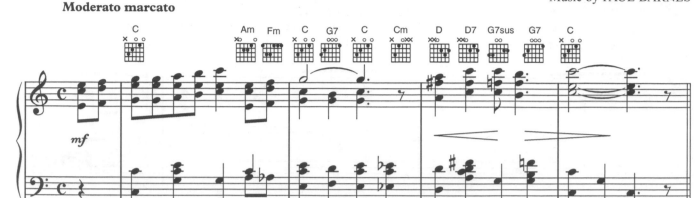

"I have come to say good-bye, Dol-ly Gray_____ It's no
Hear the roll-ing of the drums, Dol-ly Gray_____ Back from

use to ask me why, Dol-ly Gray_____ There's a mur-mur in the air you can
war the reg-'ment comes, Dol-ly Gray_____ On your love-ly face so fair I can

hear it ev – 'ry –where, it is time to do and dare, Dol – ly Gray_____ Don't you
see a look of care for your sol – dier boy's not there, Dol – ly Gray_____ For the

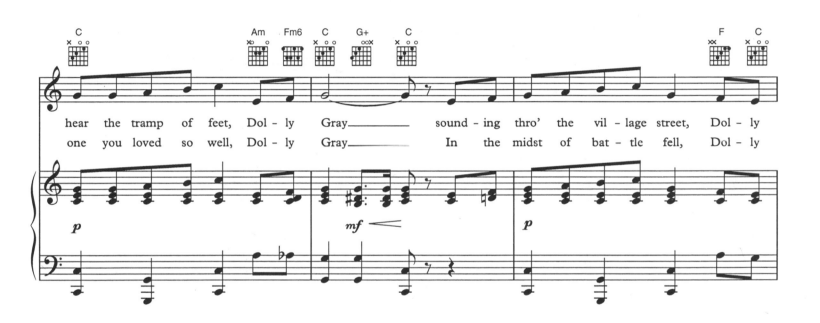

hear the tramp of feet, Dol – ly Gray_____ sound – ing thro' the vil – lage street, Dol – ly
one you loved so well, Dol – ly Gray_____ In the midst of bat – tle fell, Dol – ly

Gray_____ 'Tis the tramp of sol – dier's feet in their un – i –forms so neat "So good-
Gray_____ With his face to –wards the foe as he died he mur –mured low, "I must

ing, and I can no long – er stay._____ Hark! I

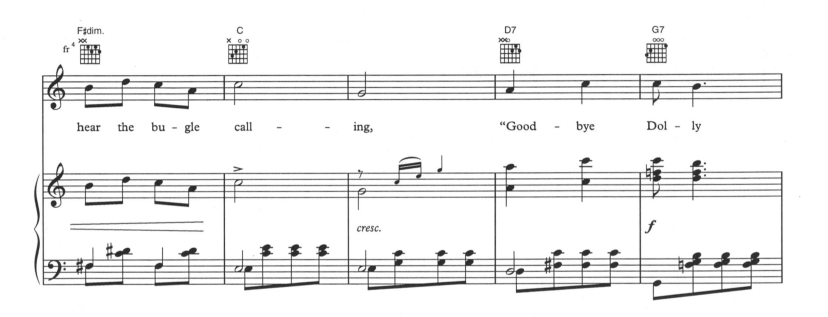

hear the bu – gle call – – ing, "Good – bye Dol – ly

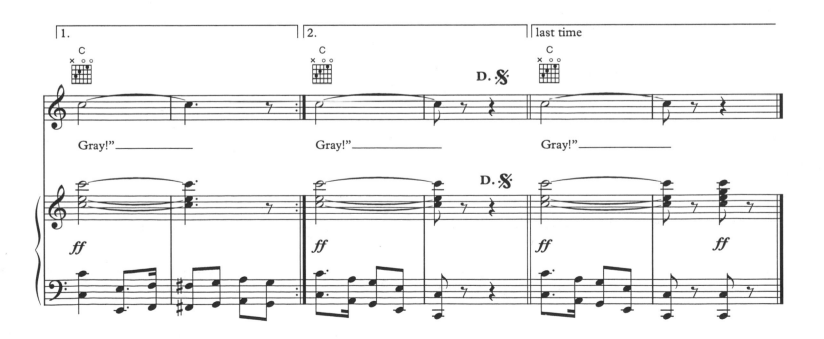

Gray!"_____ Gray!"_____ Gray!"_____

THE HONEYSUCKLE AND THE BEE

Steady tempo

Words by ALBERT H FITZ
Music by WILLIAM PENN

BECAUSE

French Words by GUY D'HARDELOT
English Words by EDWARD TESCHEMACHER
Music by GUY D'HARDELOT

TWO LITTLE BOYS

Words by EDWARD MADDEN
Music by THEODORE MORSE

I DO LIKE TO BE BESIDE THE SEASIDE

Words and Music by JOHN A GLOVER-KIND

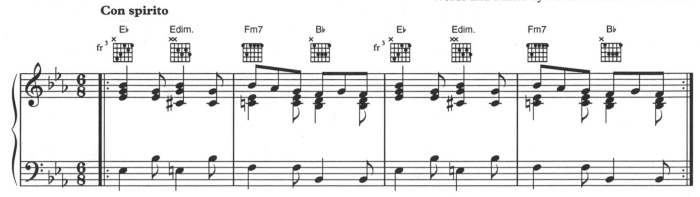

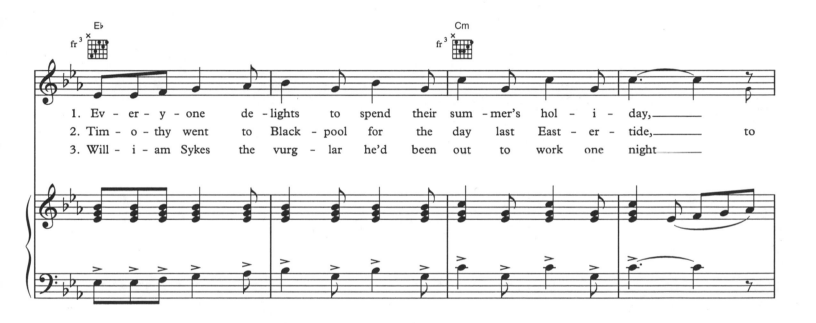

1. Ev - er - y - one de - lights to spend their sum - mer's hol - i - day,____ Ev -
2. Tim - o - thy went to Black - pool for the day last East - er - tide,____ to
3. Will - i - am Sykes the vurg - lar he'd been out to work one night____

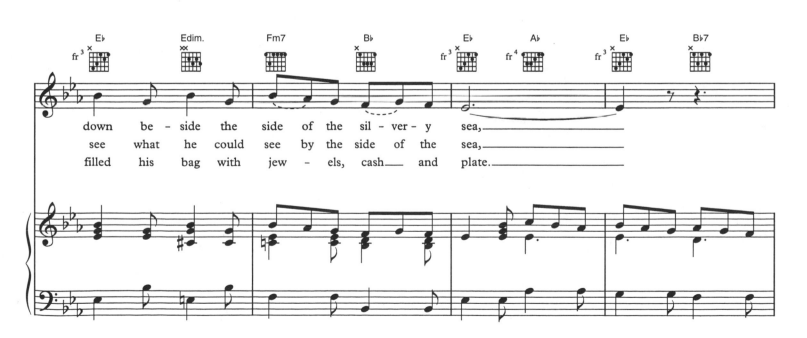

down be - side the side of the sil - ver - y sea,____
see what he could see by the side of the sea,____
filled his bag with jew - els, cash___ and plate.____

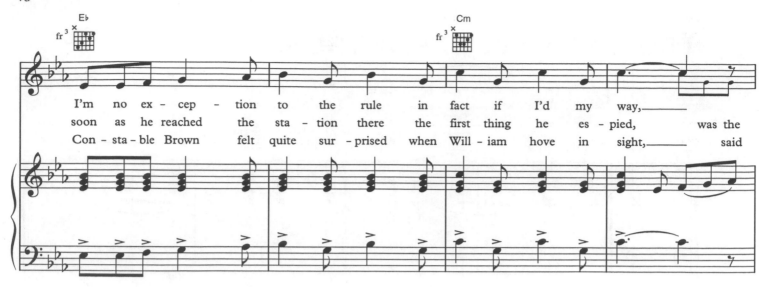

I'm no ex - cep - tion to the rule in fact if I'd my way,_____
soon as he reached the sta - tion there the first thing he es - pied, was the
Con - sta - ble Brown felt quite sur - prised when Will - iam hove in sight,_____ said

I'd re - side by the side of the sil - ver - y sea,_____ but
wine lodge door stood op - en in - vit - ing - ly,_____ to
he "The hours___ you're keep - ing are far___ too late",_____ So he

when you're just a com - mon or gar - den work - ing lad like me,_____ a
quench his thirst he tod - dled in - side and called out for a 'wine',_____ which
grabbed him by the col - lar and lodged him safe and sound in jail._____ Next

Bb7   Eb

chance to see the sea_____ is quite a nov - el - ty,_____ I
grew to eight or nine_____ 'til his nose be - gan to shine,_____ said
morn - ing look - ing pale_____ Bill told a tear - ful tale,_____ the

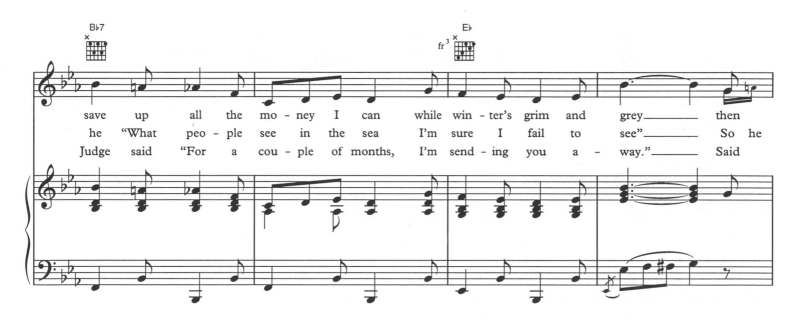

Bb7   Eb

save up all the mo - ney I can while win - ter's grim and grey_____ then
he "What peo - ple see in the sea I'm sure I fail to see"_____ So he
Judge said "For a cou - ple of months, I'm send - ing you a - way."_____ Said

Gm6   Bb   F7   Bb7

off I run to have some fun where the bal - my bree - zes play.
caught the train back home a - gain then___ to his wife said he. } Oh! I
Bill "How kind." Well if you don't mind where I spend my hol - i - day.

GIVE MY REGARDS TO BROADWAY

Tempo di marcia

Words and Music by GEORGE M COHAN

mail;_____ I___ told them I was on my way to
me;_____ Men-tion my name ev-'ry place you go, to

old Man-hat-tan Isle;_____ They all gath-ered a-bout, as the
'round the town you roam;_____ Wish you'd call on my gal, now re-

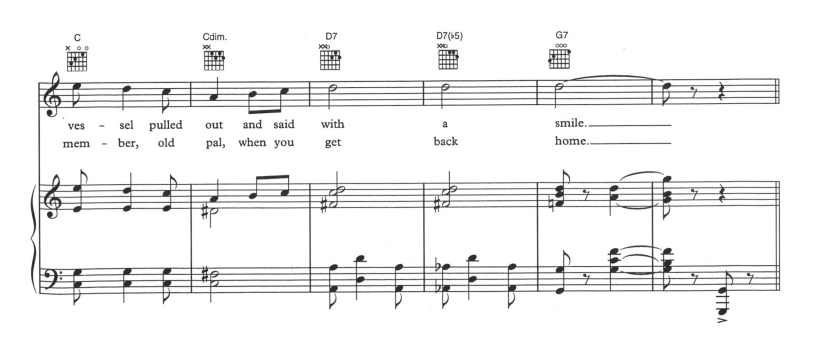

ves-sel pulled out and said with a smile._____
mem-ber, old pal, when you get back home._____

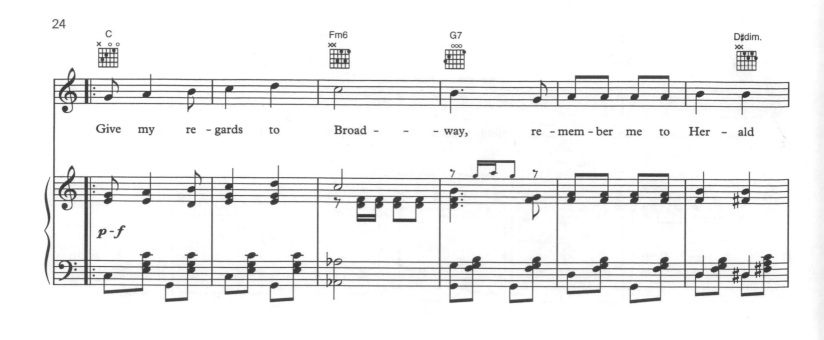

Give my re -gards to Broad - - -way, re -mem -ber me to Her - ald

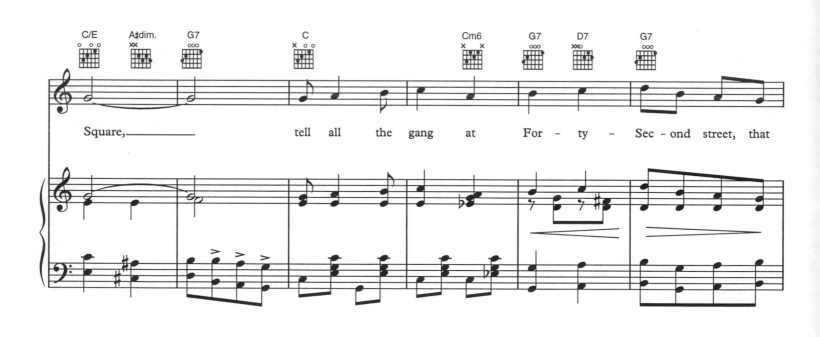

Square,_____ tell all the gang at For - ty - Sec -ond street, that

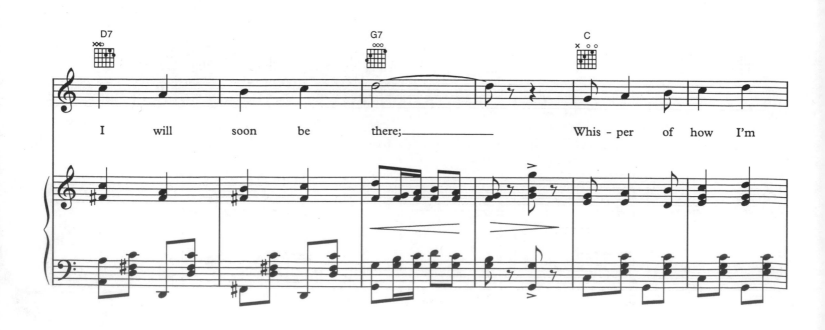

I will soon be there;_____ Whis - per of how I'm

yearn - - - ing to min - gle with the old time throng,_____

give my re - gards to old Broad - way and say that I'll be

there e'er long._____ long._____

IN THE SHADE OF THE OLD APPLE TREE

Words by HARRY WILLIAMS
Music by EGBERT VAN ALSTYNE

hear the dull buzz of the bee_____ in the blos -soms as you said to

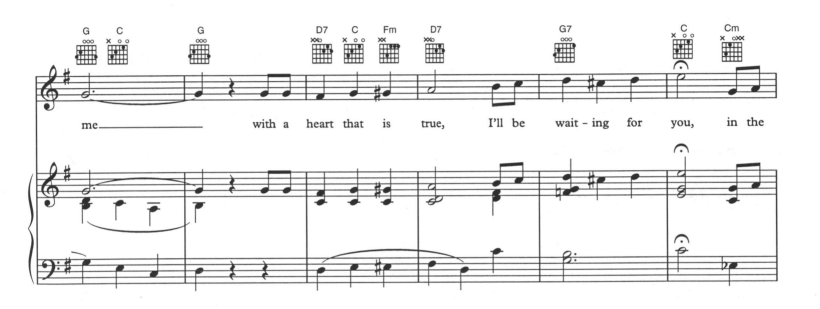

me_____ with a heart that is true, I'll be wait - ing for you, in the

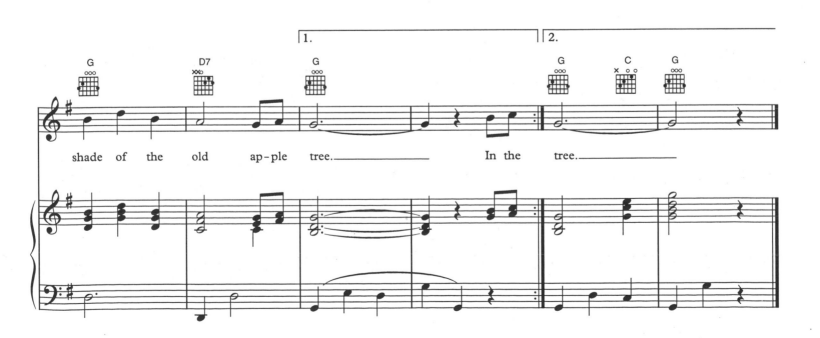

shade of the old ap -ple tree._____ In the tree._____

BY THE SIDE OF THE ZUYDER ZEE

Words by A J MILLS
Music by BENNETT SCOTT

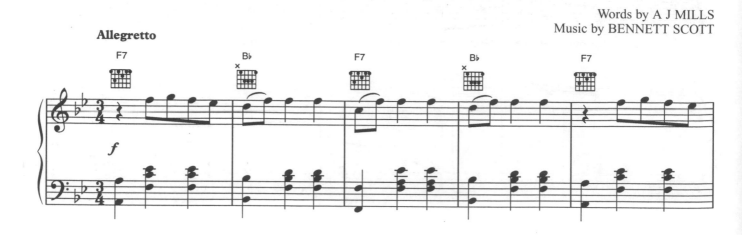

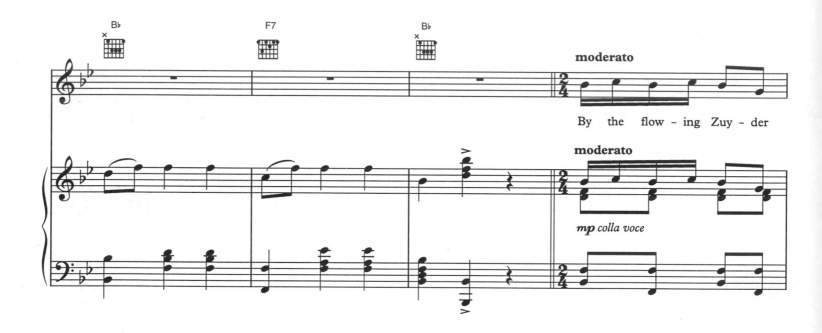

By the flow – ing Zuy – der

Zee so blue, there's a lit – tle Dutch girl I love true,

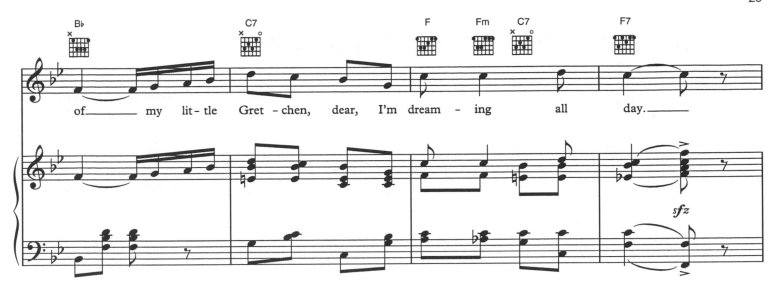

of _____ my lit- tle Gret -chen, dear, I'm dream -ing all day. _____

She's a pic -ture a -ny one would chose, in her pret -ty frock and

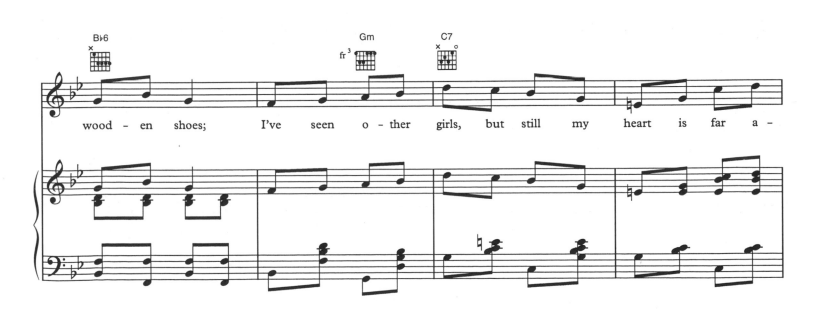

wood -en shoes; I've seen o -ther girls, but still my heart is far a-

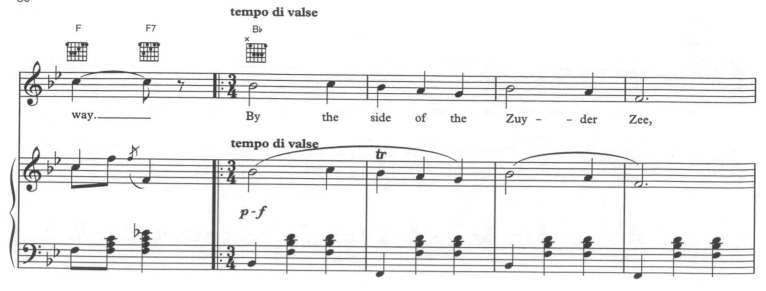

way._____ By the side of the Zuy - - der Zee,

Zuy - der Zee, Zuy - der Zee, there my Diet -cher girl

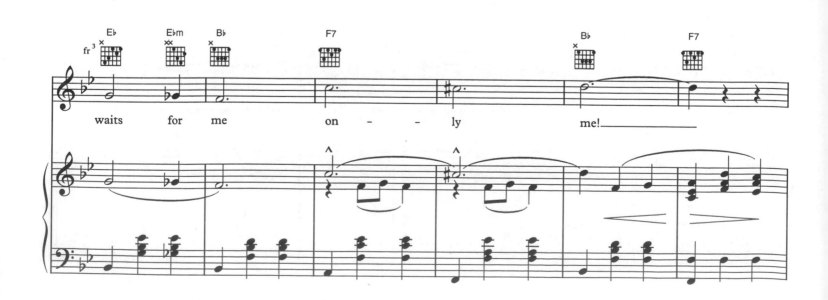

waits for me on - - ly me!_____

I've seen dia-monds in Am-ster-dam, Am-ster-dam,

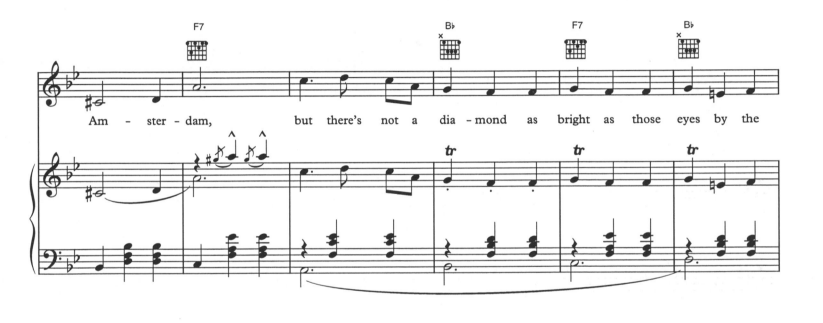

Am-ster-dam, but there's not a dia-mond as bright as those eyes by the

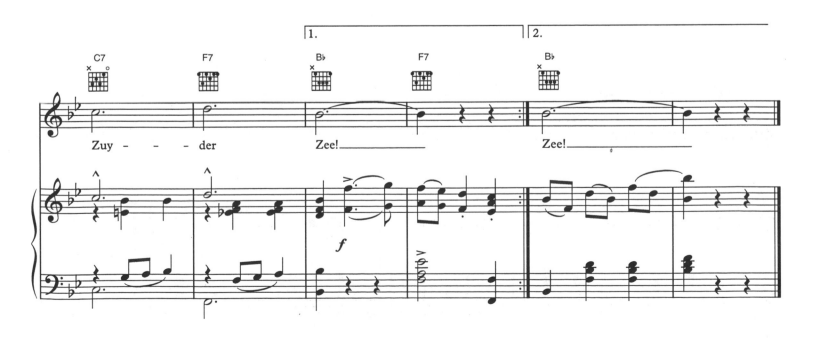

Zuy- -der Zee! Zee!

SHE'S A LASSIE FROM LANCASHIRE

Words and Music by C W MURPHY,
DAN LIPTON and JOHN NEAT

Tempo di valse

From a dear lit-tle Lan-ca-shire town, a boy had sail'd a-way_____ a - cross the brin - y spray_____ to

toil in U. S. A._____ When A - mer - i - can

girls gath - er'd round and sought his com - pa - ny,_____

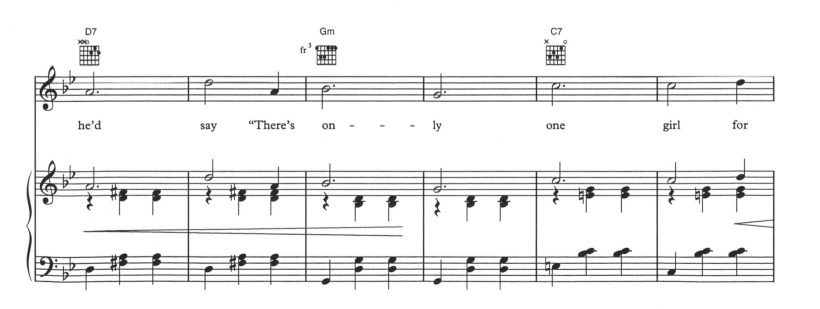

he'd say "There's on - - - ly one girl for

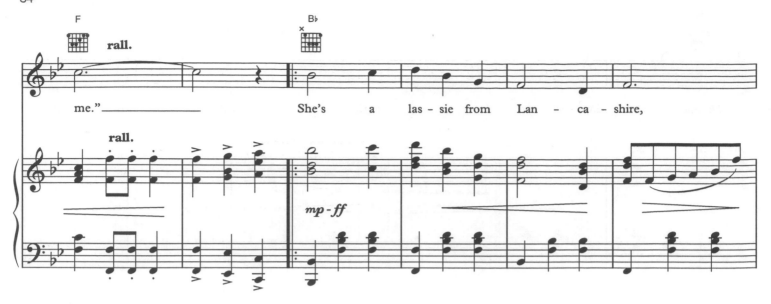

me." _____ She's a las - sie from Lan - ca - shire,

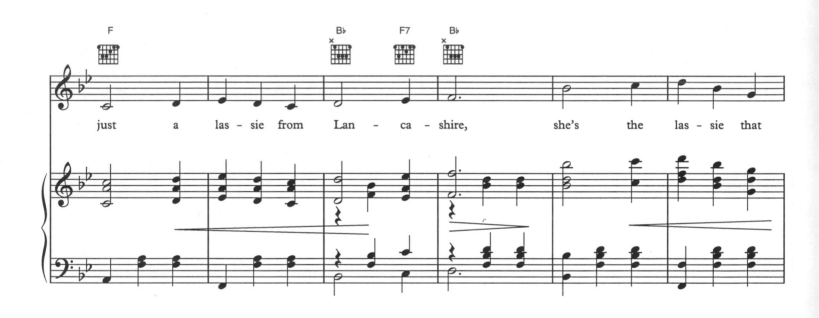

just a las - sie from Lan - ca - shire, she's the las - sie that

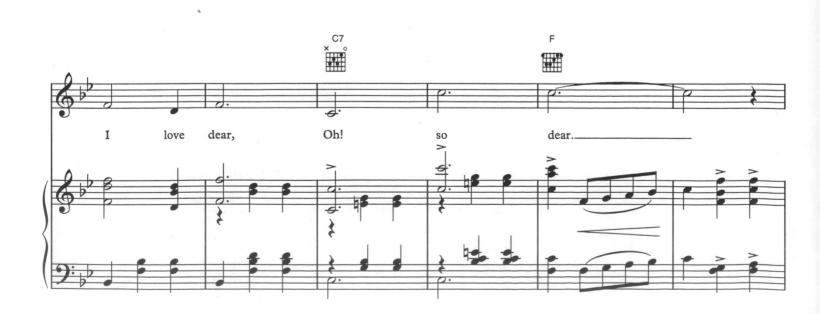

I love dear, Oh! so dear. _____

Though she dres - ses in clogs and shawl, she's the pret - ti - est

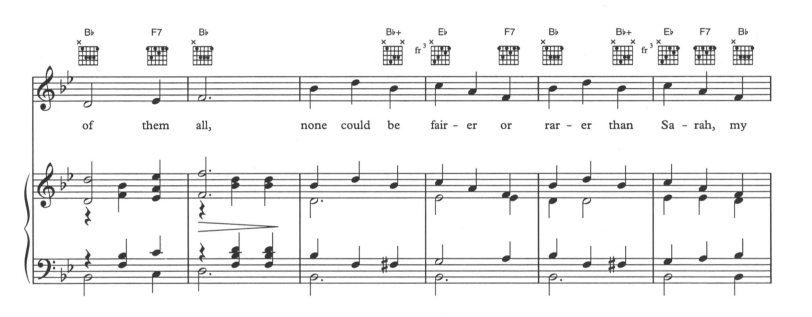

of them all, none could be fair - er or rar - er than Sa - rah, my

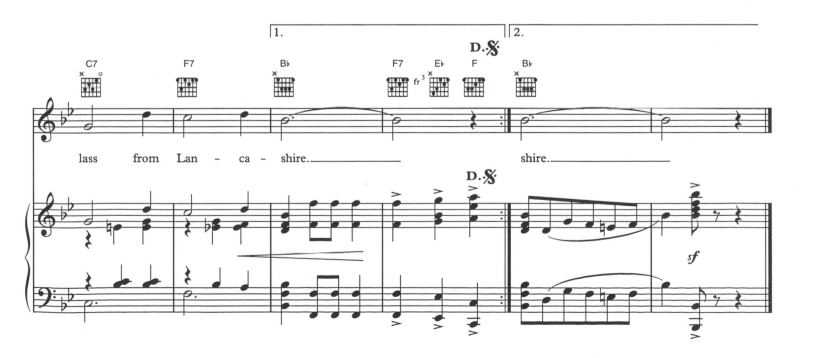

lass from Lan - ca - shire. shire.

SHINE ON HARVEST MOON

Words by JACK NORWORTH
Music by NORA BAYES

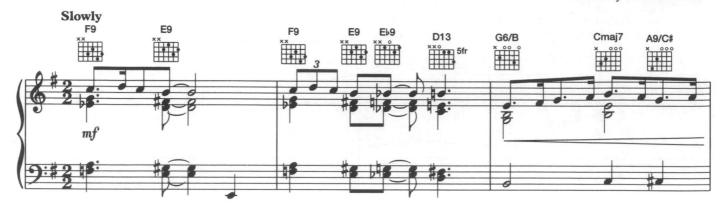

1. The night was might-y dark, so you could hard-ly see,___ for the
2. I can't see why a boy should sigh, when by his side___ is the

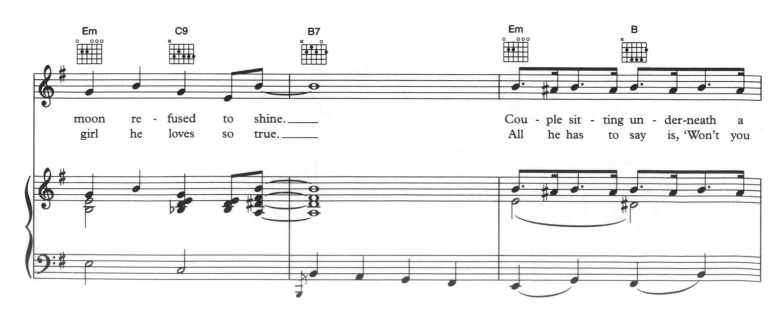

moon re-fused to shine.___ Cou-ple sit-ting un-der-neath a
girl he loves so true.___ All he has to say is, 'Won't you

I'M HENERY THE EIGHTH, I AM!

Words and Music by
FRED MURRAY and R P WESTON

Steady tempo

I'm Hen – er – y the Eighth I am!___

Hen – er – y the Eighth, I am I am!___

I got mar – ried to the wid – ow next door,

she's been mar - ried sev - en times_____ be - fore._____

Ev - - - 'ry one was a "Hen - er - y"_____ she

would - -n't have a Wil - lie or a Sam._____

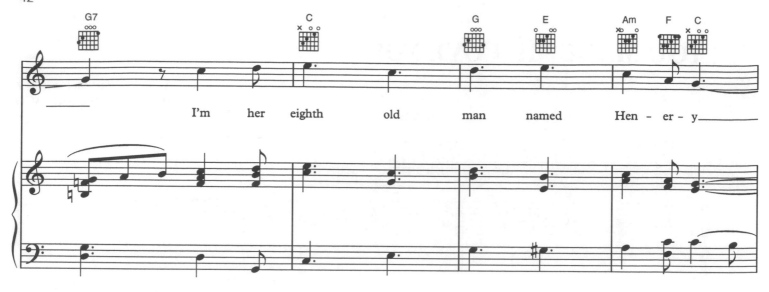

I'm her eighth old man named Hen - er - y_____

_____ I'm Hen - er - y the Eighth I

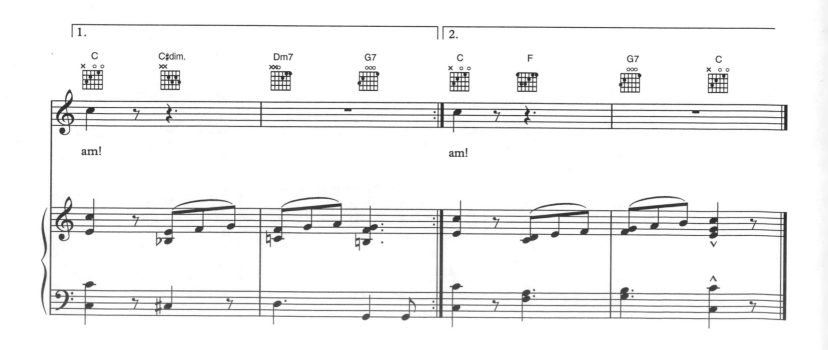

am!

am!

YOU MADE ME LOVE YOU

Words by JOE McCARTHY
Music by JAMES MONACO

1. I've been wor-ried all day long,
2. I had pic-tured in my mind,

don't know if I'm right or wrong,
some-day I would sure-ly find,

I can't help just
some-one hand-some,

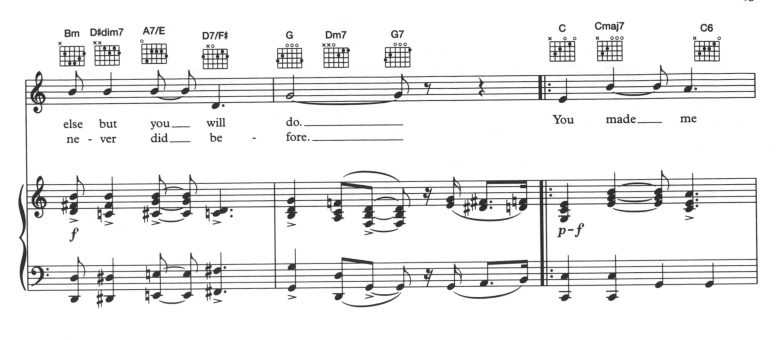

else but you___ will do._____ You made___ me
ne - ver did___ be - fore._____

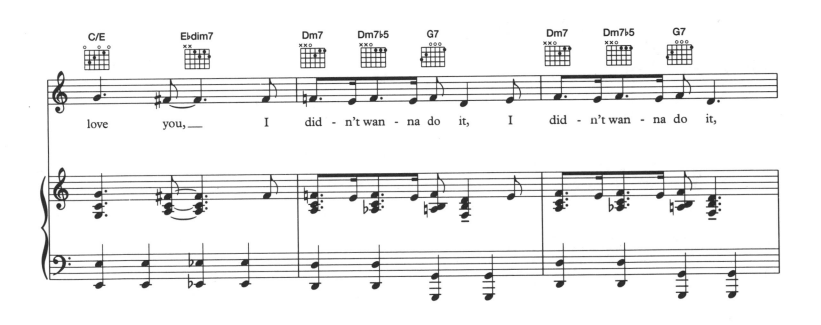

love you,___ I did - n't wan - na do it, I did - n't wan - na do it,

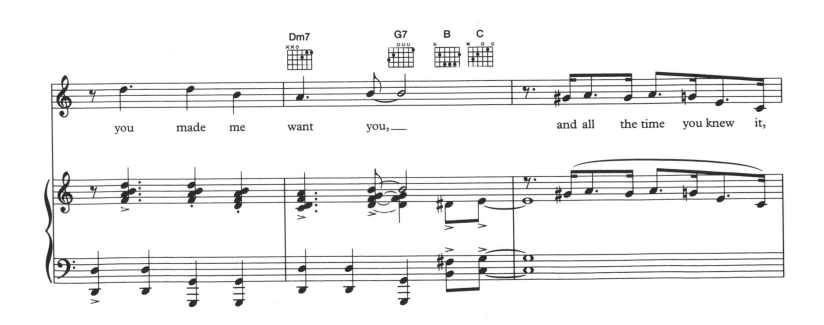

you made me want you,___ and all the time you knew it,

ANY OLD IRON

Words and Music by CHARLES COLLINS,
E A SHEPPARD and FRED TERRY

Moderato

Just a week or two a-go my poor old Un-cle Bill,
I went to the ci-ty once and thought I'd have a spree. The
Just to have a lit-tle bit of fun the oth-er day,
Shan't for-get when I got mar-ried to Se-li-na Brown. The

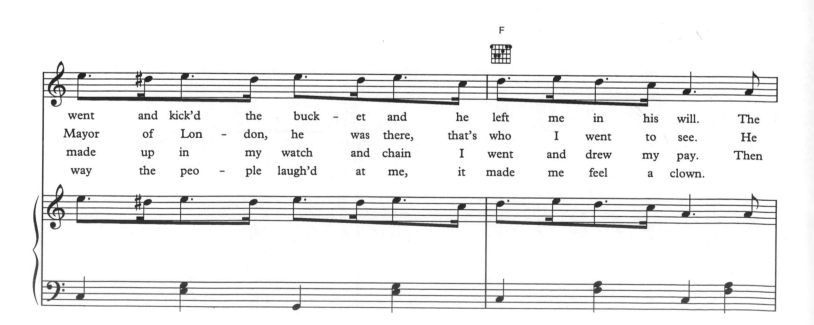

went and kick'd the buck-et and he left me in his will. The
Mayor of Lon-don, he was there, that's who I went to see. He
made up in my watch and chain I went and drew my pay. Then
way the peo-ple laugh'd at me, it made me feel a clown.

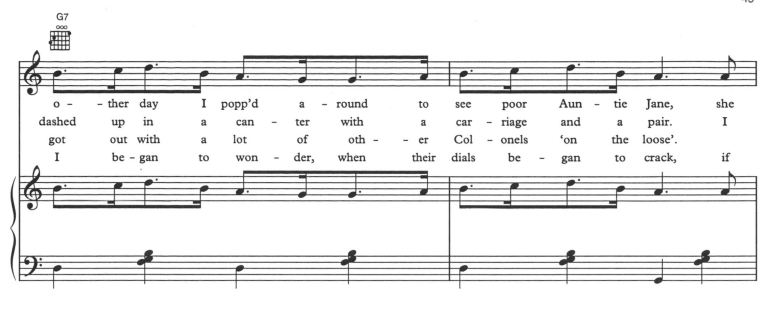

o - -ther day I popp'd a -round to see poor Aun - tie Jane, she
dashed up in a can - ter with a car - riage and a pair. I
got out with a lot of oth - -er Col - onels 'on the loose'.
I be - gan to won - der, when their dials be - gan to crack, if

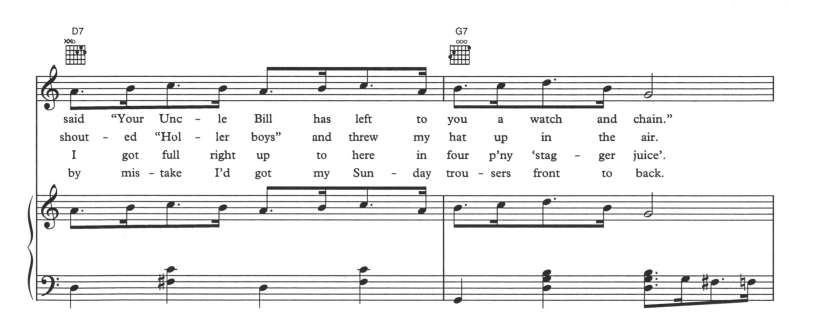

said "Your Unc - le Bill has left to you a watch and chain."
shout - ed "Hol - ler boys" and threw my hat up in the air.
I got full right up to here in four p'ny 'stag - ger juice'.
by mis - take I'd got my Sun - day trou - sers front to back.

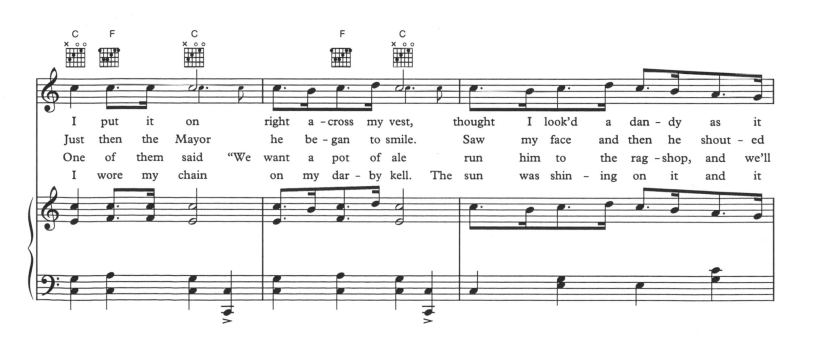

I put it on right a - cross my vest, thought I look'd a dan - dy as it
Just then the Mayor he be - gan to smile. Saw my face and then he shout - ed
One of them said "We want a pot of ale run him to the rag - shop, and we'll
I wore my chain on my dar - by kell. The sun was shin - ing on it and it

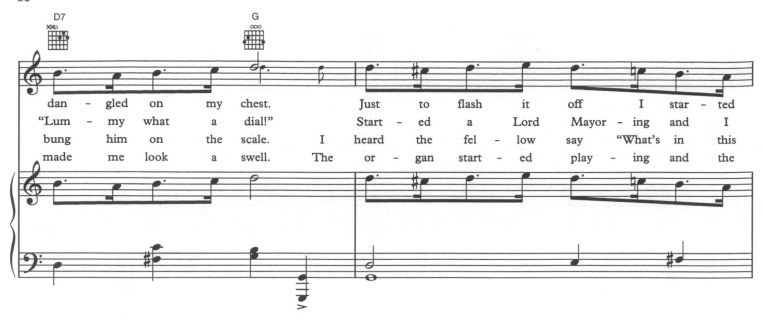

dan - gled on my chest. Just to flash it off I star - ted
"Lum - my what a dial!" Start - ed a Lord Mayor - ing and I
made me look a swell. The or - gan start - ed play - ing and the

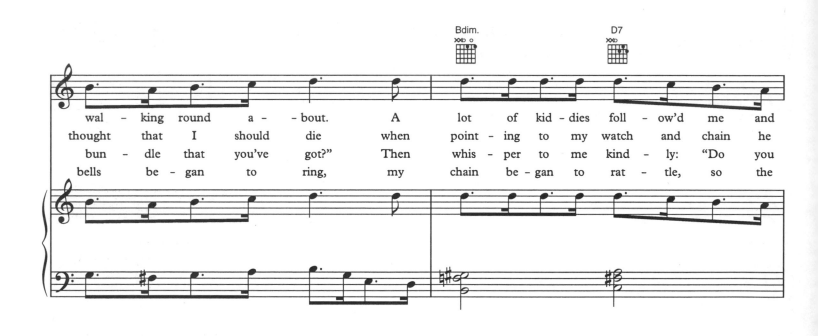

wal - king round a - -bout. A lot of kid - dies foll - ow'd me and
thought that I should die when point - ing to my watch and chain he
bun - dle that you've got?" Then whis - per to me kind - ly: "Do you
bells be - gan to ring, my chain be - gan to rat - tle, so the

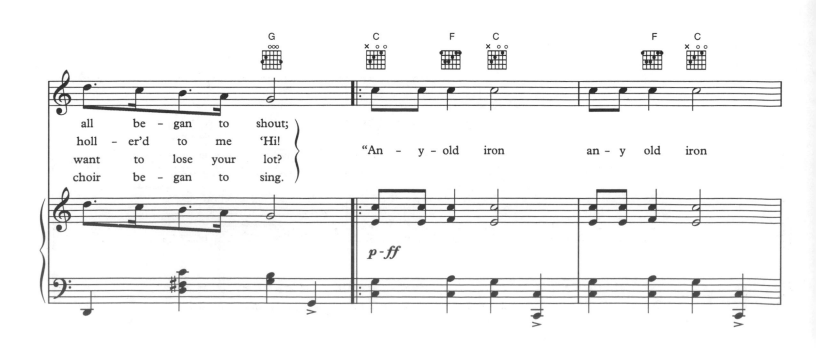

all be - gan to shout;
holl - er'd to me 'Hi!
want to lose your lot?
choir be - gan to sing.

"An - y - old iron an - y old iron

p-ff

WHEN IRISH EYES ARE SMILING

Words by CHAUNCEY OLCOTT and GEORGE GRAFF
Music by ERNEST R BALL

KEEP THE HOME FIRES BURNING

Words by LENA GUILBERT FORD
Music by IVOR NOVELLO

PACK UP YOUR TROUBLES (IN YOUR OLD KIT BAG)

Words by GEORGE ASAF
Music by FELIX POWELL

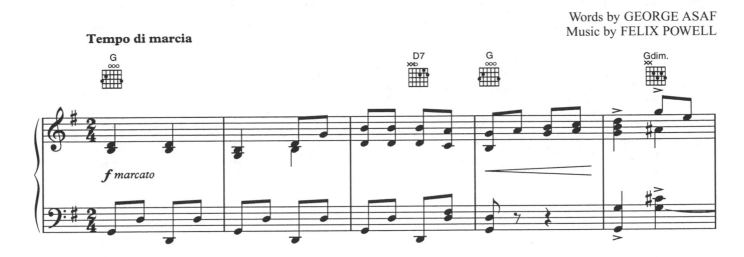

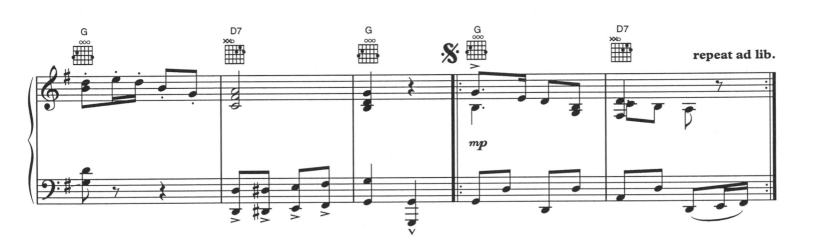

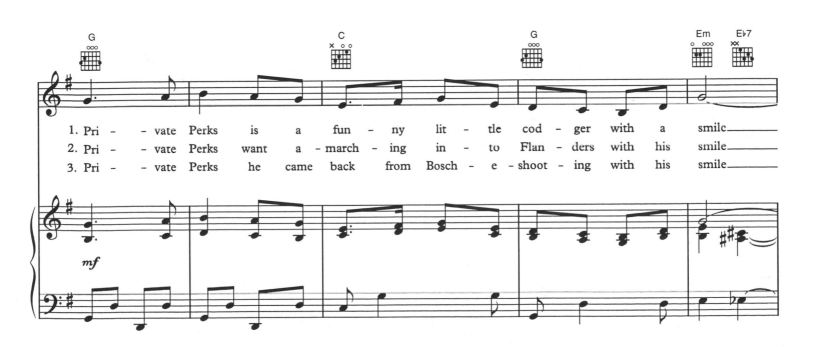

1. Pri - - vate Perks is a fun - ny lit - tle cod - ger with a smile____
2. Pri - - vate Perks want a - march - ing in - to Flan - ders with his smile____
3. Pri - - vate Perks he came back from Bosch - e - shoot - ing with his smile____

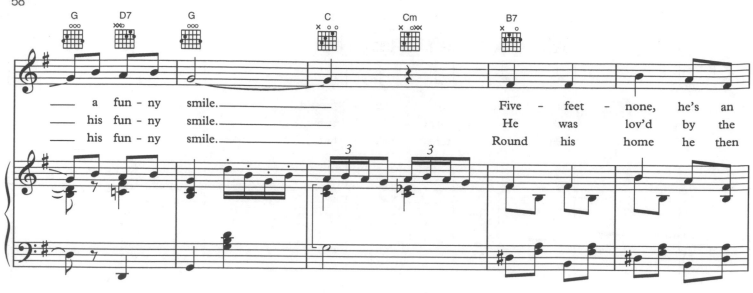

_____ a fun-ny smile._____ Five-feet-none, he's an
_____ his fun-ny smile._____ He was lov'd by the
_____ his fun-ny smile._____ Round his home he then

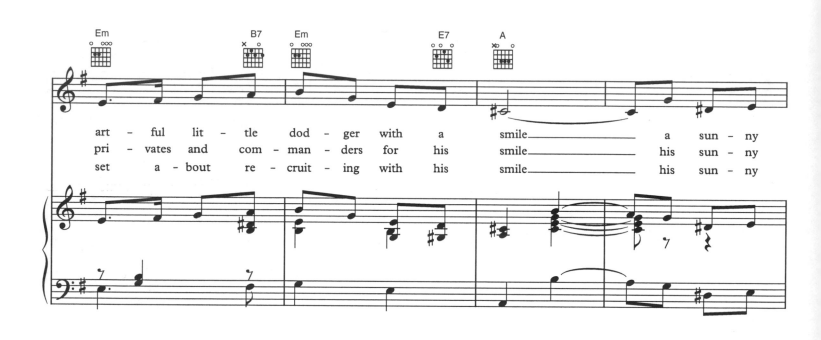

art-ful lit-tle dod-ger with a smile_____ a sun-ny
pri-vates and com-man-ders for his smile_____ his sun-ny
set a-bout re-cruit-ing with his smile_____ his sun-ny

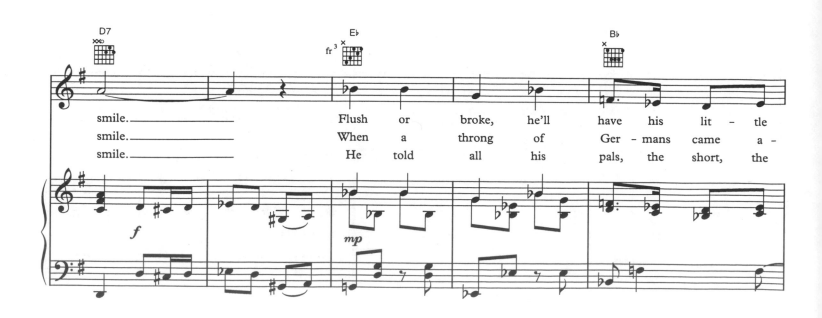

smile._____ Flush or broke, he'll have his lit-tle
smile._____ When a throng of Ger-mans came a-
smile._____ He told all his pals, the short, the

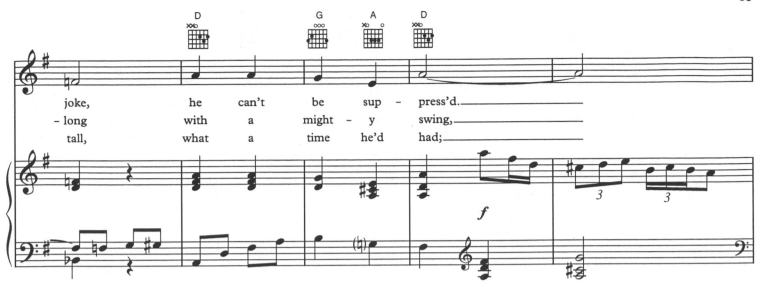

joke,   he can't be sup- press'd._____
-long   with a might- y swing,_____
tall,   what a time he'd had;_____

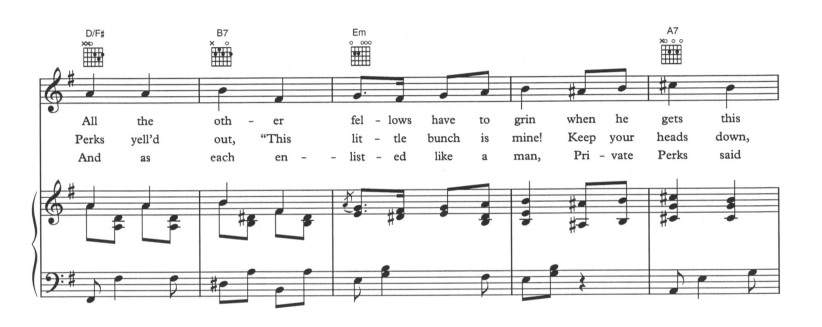

All   the   oth - er   fel - lows have to grin when he gets this
Perks yell'd out, "This lit - tle bunch is mine! Keep your heads down,
And   as   each en - list - ed like a man, Pri - vate Perks said

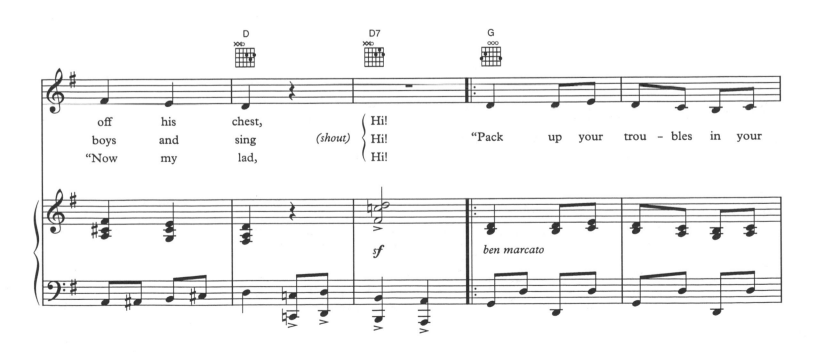

off   his   chest,   *(shout)*   Hi!
boys   and   sing   Hi!   "Pack up your trou - bles in your
"Now   my   lad,   Hi!

sf   *ben marcato*

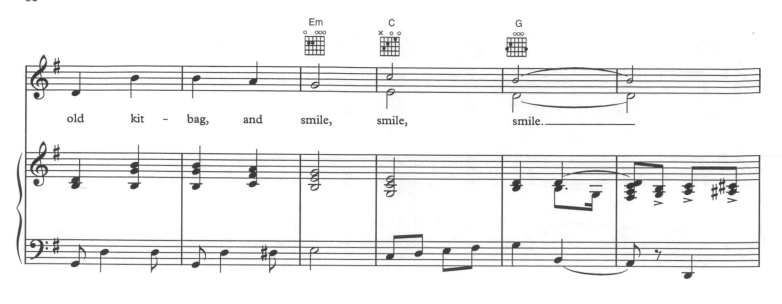

old kit - bag, and smile, smile, smile._____

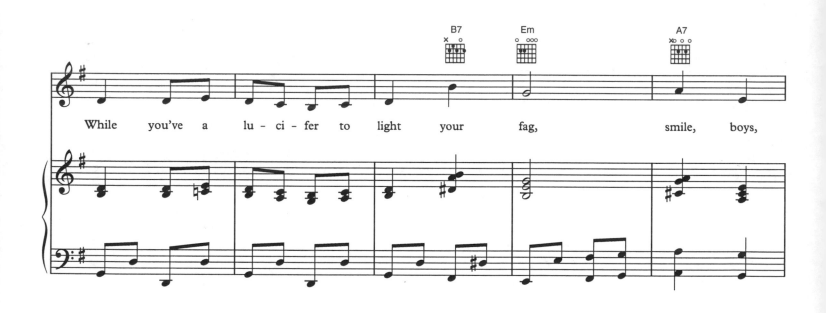

While you've a lu - ci - fer to light your fag, smile, boys,

that's the style._____ What's the use of

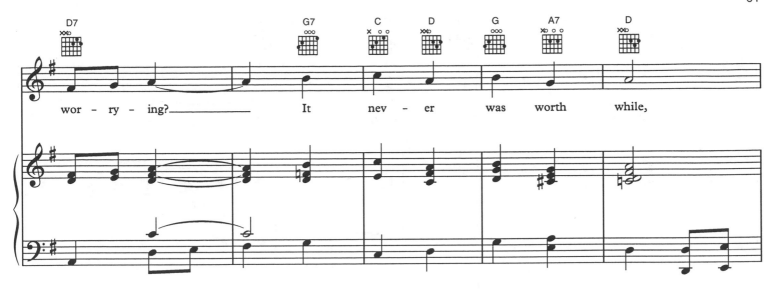

wor – ry – ing?_____ It nev – er was worth while,

so pack up your trou – bles in your old kit – bag, and

smile, smile, smile."_____ smile."_____ (fine)

IF YOU WERE THE ONLY GIRL IN THE WORLD

Words by CLIFFORD GREY
Music by NAT D AYER

I'M FOREVER BLOWING BUBBLES

Words and Music by
JAAN KENBROVIN and JOHN KELLETTE

FOR ME AND MY GIRL

Words by EDGAR LESLIE and E RAY GOETZ
Music by GEORGE W MEYER

joy,_____ he's the luck - i - est boy,_____ in his wed-ding ar -
sight_____ as the fam-ilies u - nite._____ Gee! it makes the boy

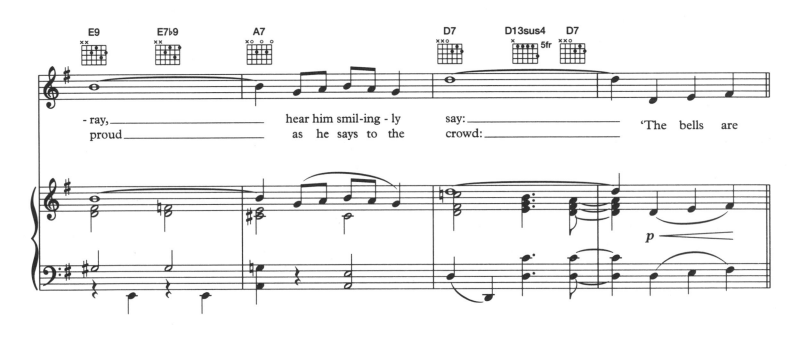

- ray,_____ hear him smil-ing - ly say:_____ 'The bells are
proud_____ as he says to the crowd:_____

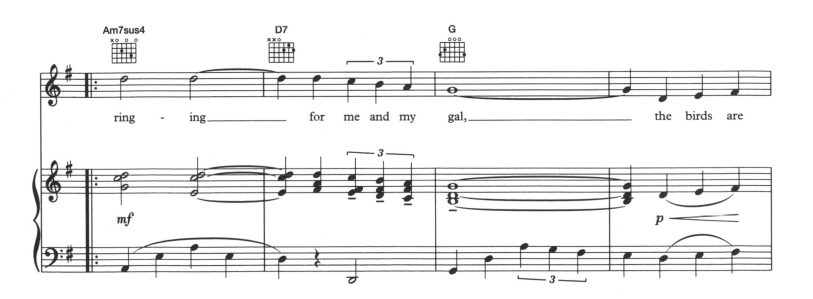

ring - ing_____ for me and my gal,_____ the birds are

AFTER YOU'VE GONE

Words and Music by
HENRY CREAMER and TURNER LAYTON

AVALON

Words by AL JOLSON and BUDDY DeSYLVA
Music by VINCENT ROSE

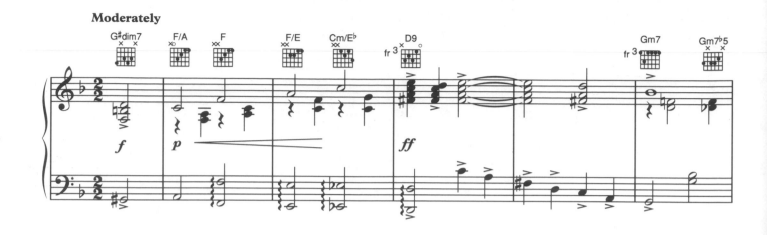

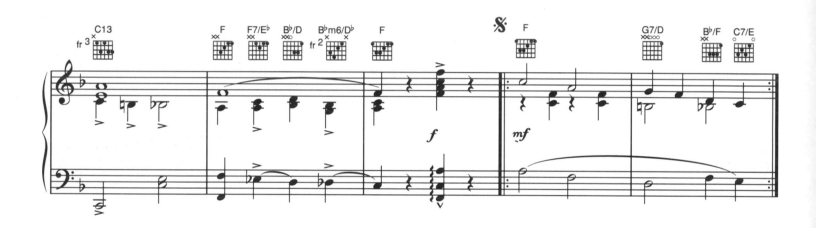

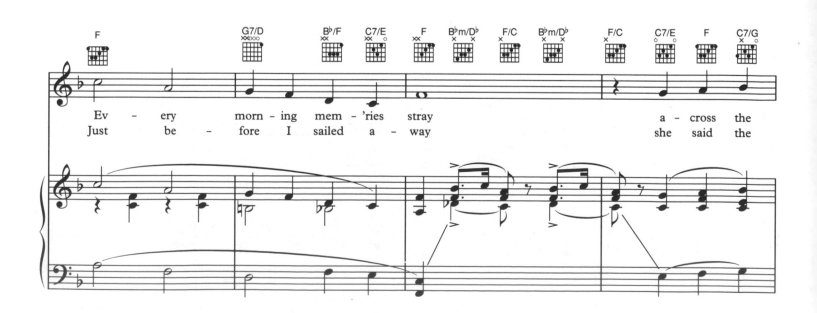

Ev — ery morn – ing mem – 'ries stray
Just be – fore I sailed a – way

a – cross the
she said the

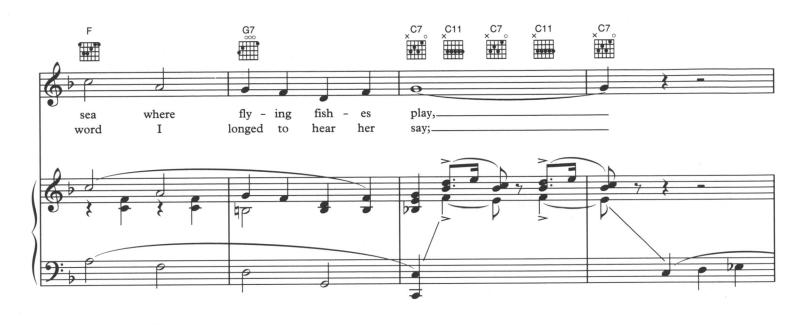

sea   where   fly - ing fish - es   play,_____
word   I   longed to hear   her   say;_____

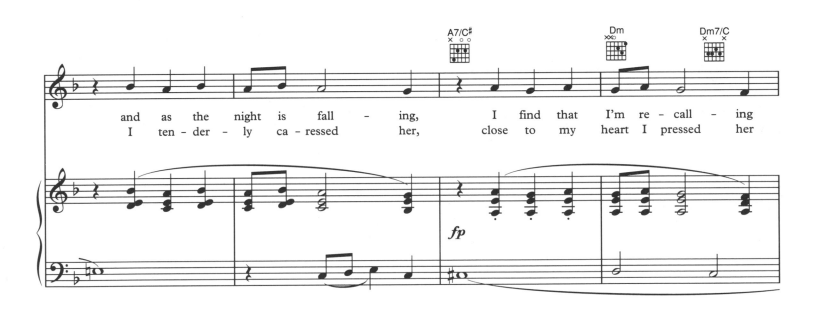

and   as   the   night is   fall - ing,   I   find that   I'm re - call - ing
I   ten - der - ly ca - ressed   her,   close to my heart I pressed her

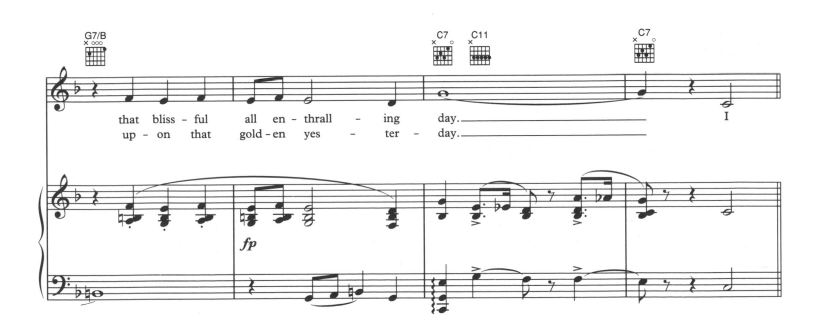

that bliss - ful all en - thrall - ing   day._____
up - on that gold - en yes - ter - day._____   I

APRIL SHOWERS

Words by BUDDY DeSYLVA
Music by LOUIS SILVERS

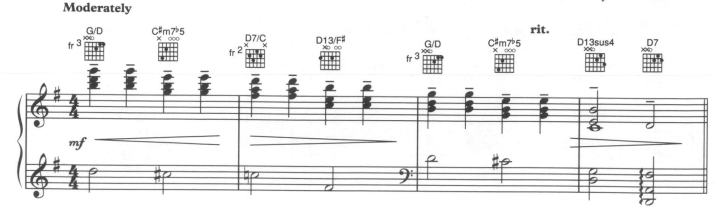

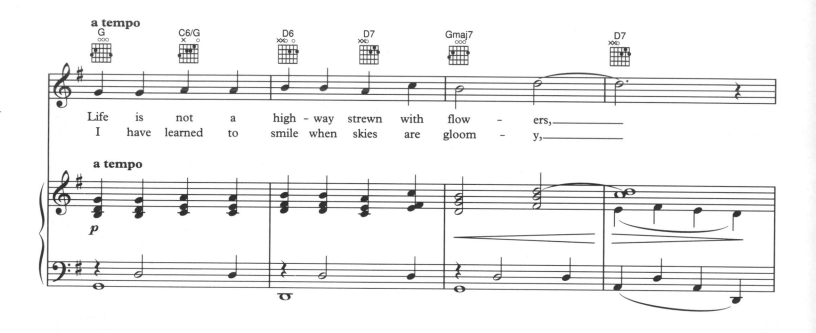

Life is not a high - way strewn with flow - ers,_____
I have learned to smile when skies are gloom - y,_____

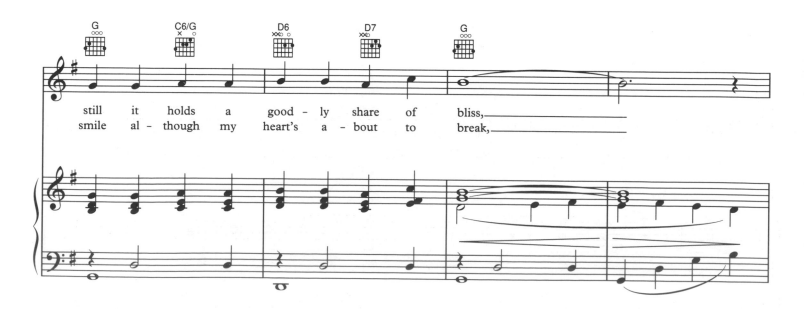

still it holds a good - ly share of bliss,_____
smile al - though my heart's a - bout to break,_____

_____ of daf - fo - dils, _____ so keep on look - ing for a blue - bird and

list - 'ning for his song, when - ev - er A - pril show - ers come a -

-long. _____ Through A - pril -long. _____

CHICAGO

Words and Music by FRED FISHER

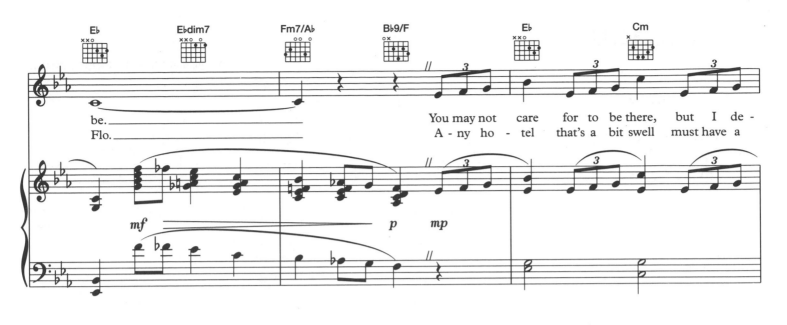

be. _____ You may not care for to be there, but I de-
Flo. _____ A - ny ho - tel that's a bit swell must have a

- clare, you're not a - ware just where to go. _____ When you're in
band right here on hand or else they're cheap. _____ If you'll in -

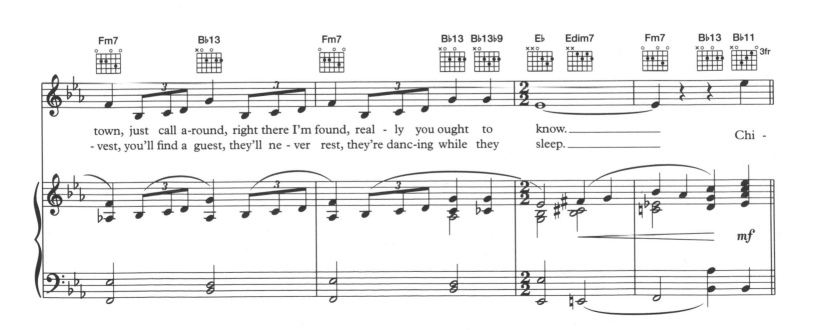

town, just call a-round, right there I'm found, real - ly you ought to know. _____ Chi -
- vest, you'll find a guest, they'll ne - ver rest, they're danc-ing while they sleep. _____

IT HAD TO BE YOU

Words by GUS KAHN
Music by ISHAM JONES

WHO'S SORRY NOW

Words by BERT KALMAR and HARRY RUBY
Music by TED SNYDER

HOW LONG HAS THIS BEEN GOING ON?

Music and Lyrics by
GEORGE GERSHWIN and IRA GERSHWIN

Bill: As a tot, when I trot-ted in lit-tle vel-vet pant - ies,___
Mary: 'Neath the stars at ba-zaars of-ten I've had to ca-ress men,___

I was kissed by my sis-ters, my cou-sins and my aunt - ies.___
Five or ten dol-lars then I'd col-lect from all those yes - men.___

YES SIR, THAT'S MY BABY

Words by GUS KAHN
Music by WALTER DONALDSON

SOMEONE TO WATCH OVER ME

Music and Lyrics by
GEORGE GERSHWIN and IRA GERSHWIN

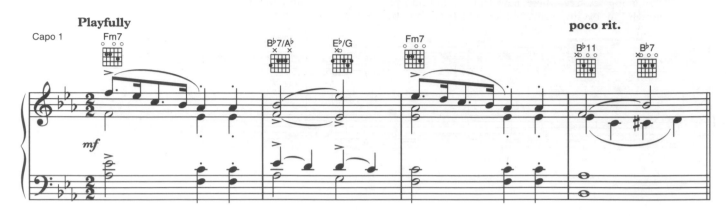

There's a say-ing old, says that love is blind. Still we're of-ten told, 'Seek and ye shall find.'
When you're all a-lone, life is ne-ver gay and I've got to own things are look-ing grey.

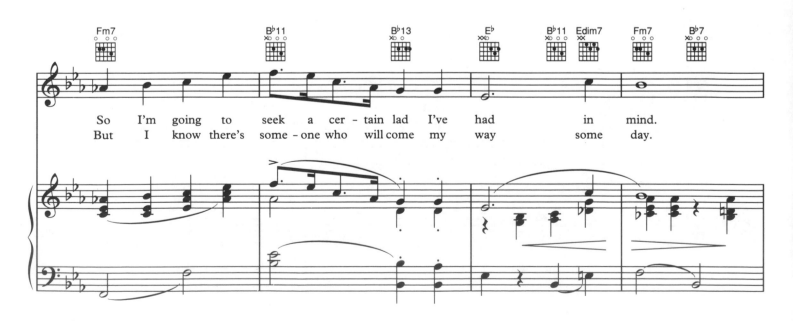

So I'm going to seek a cer-tain lad I've had in mind.
But I know there's some-one who will come my way some day.

LET'S DO IT (LET'S FALL IN LOVE)

Words and Music by COLE PORTER

When the lit-tle blue-bird, who has ne-ver said a word, starts to sing: 'Spring, spring' when the

lit-tle blue-bell, in the bot-tom of the dell, starts to ring: 'Ding, ding' when the

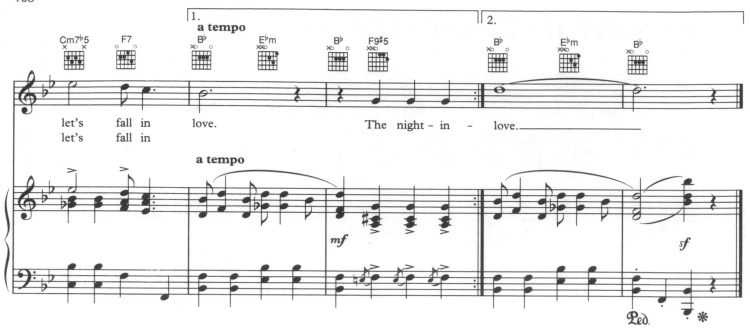

let's fall in love. The night - in - love.
let's fall in

Verse 1:

Mr Irving Berlin
Often emphasizes sin
In a charming way
Mr Coward we know
Wrote a song or two to show
Sex was here to stay
Richard Rodgers it's true
Takes a more romantic view
Of that sly biological urge
But it really was Cole
Who contrived to make the whole
Thing merge

Verse 2:

In the Spring of the year
Inhibitions disappear
And our hearts beat high
We had better face the facts
Every gland that overacts
Has an alibi
For each bird and each bee
Each slap-happy sappy tree
Each temptation that lures us along
Is just nature elle-même
Merely singing us the same
Old song

Refrain 1:

He said that Belgians and Dutch do it
Even Hildegarde and Hutch do it
Let's do it, let's fall in love
Monkeys whenever you look do it
Aly Khan and King Farouk do it
Let's do it, let's fall in love
The most recherché cocottes do it
In a luxury flat
Locks, Dunns and Scotts do it
At the drop of a hat
Excited spinsters in spas do it
Duchesses when opening bazaars do it
Let's do it, let's fall in love

Refrain 3:

Girls from the R.A.D.A. do it
B.B.C. announcers may do it
Let's do it, let's fall in love
The Ballet Russe to a man do it
Alfred Lunt and Lynn Fontanne do it
Let's do it, let's fall in love
My kith and kin, more or less, do it
Every uncle and aunt
But I confess to it
I've one cousin who can't
Critics as sour as quince do it
Even Emile Littler and Prince do it
Let's do it, let's fall in love

Refrain 2:

Our leading writers in swarms do it
Somerset and all the Maughams do it
Let's do it, let's fall in love
The Brontës felt that they must do it
Mrs Humphry Ward could just do it
Let's do it, let's fall in love
Anouilh and Sartre - God knows why - do it
As a sort of curse
Eliot and Fry do it
But they do it in verse
Some mystics, as a routine do it
Even Evelyn Waugh and Graham Greene do it
Let's do it, let's fall in love

Refrain 4:

The House of Commons en bloc do it
Civil servants by the clock do it
Let's do it, let's fall in love
Deacons who've done it before do it
Minor canons with a roar do it
Let's do it, let's fall in love
Some rather rorty old rips do it
When they get a bit tight
Government Whips do it
If it takes them all night
Old mountain goats in ravines do it
Probably we'll live to see machines do it
Let's do it, let's fall in love

MY BABY JUST CARES FOR ME

Words by GUS KAHN
Music by WALTER DONALDSON

My ba-by don't care_____ for cars

— and__ ra - ces Ba - by don't care for,

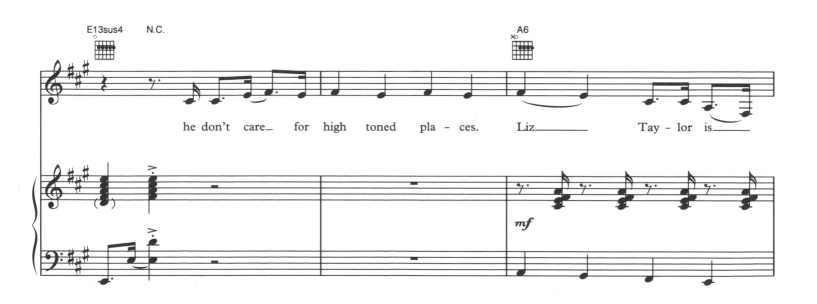

he don't care__ for high toned pla - ces. Liz_____ Tay - lor is_____

BASIN STREET BLUES

Words and Music by SPENCER WILLIAMS

DREAM A LITTLE DREAM OF ME

Words by GUS KAHN
Music by WILBUR SCHWANDT and FABIAN ANDRE

OVER THE RAINBOW

Words by E Y HARBURG
Music by HAROLD ARLEN

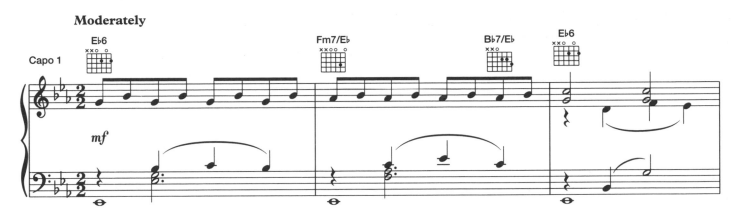

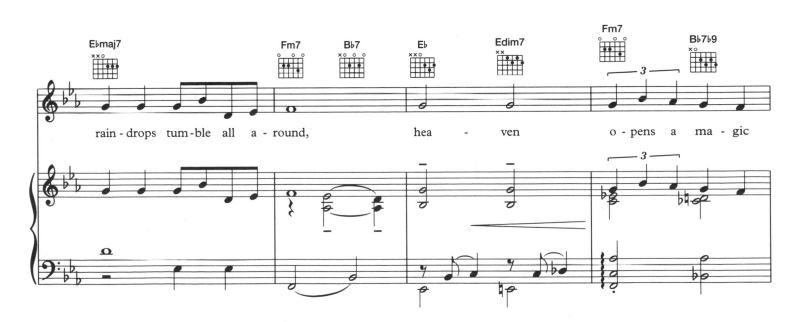

IT DON'T MEAN A THING
(IF IT AIN'T GOT THAT SWING)

Words by IRVING MILLS
Music by DUKE ELLINGTON

STORMY WEATHER

Words by TED KOEHLER
Music by HAROLD ARLEN

I GET A KICK OUT OF YOU

Words and Music by COLE PORTER

SUMMERTIME

Music and Lyrics by
GEORGE GERSHWIN, DUBOSE and
DOROTHY HEYWARD and IRA GERSHWIN

143

THE WAY YOU LOOK TONIGHT

Words by DOROTHY FIELDS
Music by JEROME KERN

MY FUNNY VALENTINE

Words by LORENZ HART
Music by RICHARD RODGERS

Be - hold the way our fine-fea-thered friend his vir-tue doth pa-rade. Thou know-est not, my dim-wit-ted friend, the pic-ture thou hast made. Thy

MOONLIGHT SERENADE

Words by MITCHELL PARISH
Music by GLENN MILLER

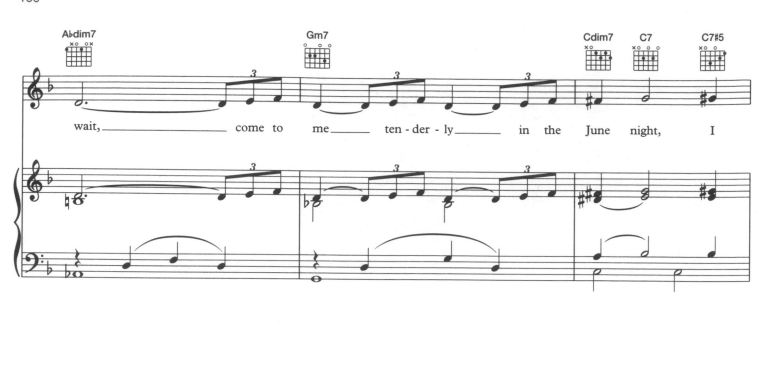

wait,_____ come to me_____ ten-der-ly_____ in the June night, I

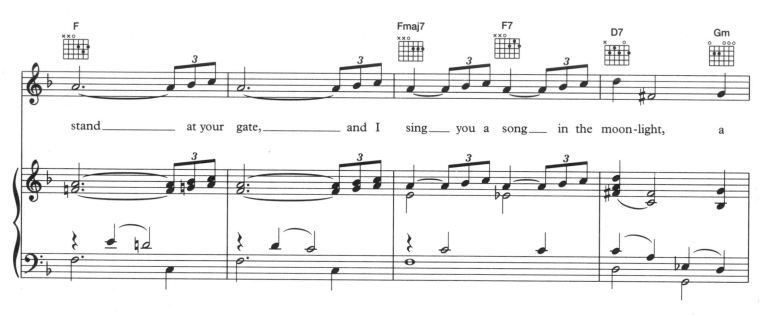

stand_____ at your gate,_____ and I sing___ you a song___ in the moon-light, a

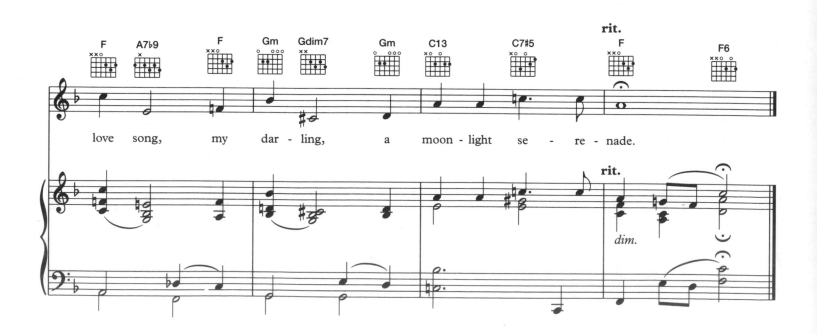

love song, my dar - ling, a moon-light se - re - nade.

DON'T GET AROUND MUCH ANYMORE

Words by BOB RUSSELL
Music by DUKE ELLINGTON

A NIGHTINGALE SANG IN BERKELEY SQUARE

Words by ERIC MASCHWITZ
Music by MANNING SHERWIN

LET THERE BE LOVE

Words by IAN MURRAY SEAFIELD GRANT
Music by LIONEL RAND

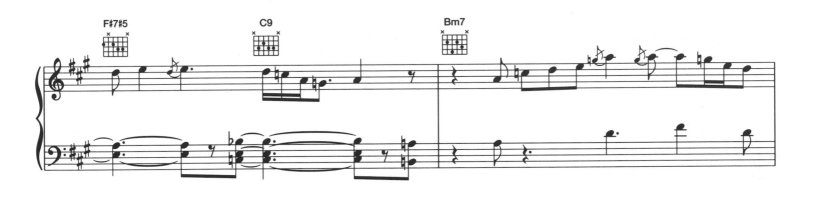

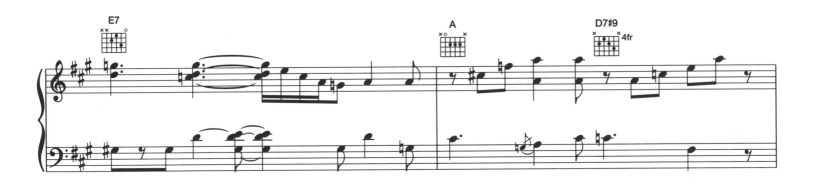

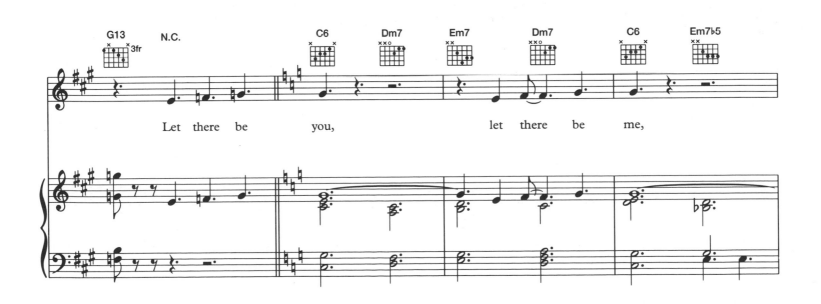

Let there be you,   let there be me,

169

Let there__ be

YOU'LL NEVER KNOW

Words by MACK GORDON
Music by HARRY WARREN

Dar-ling I'm so blue with-out you,___ I think a-bout you___ the live-long day.

When you ask me if I'm lone-ly,___ then I have on-ly this to say;

You'll ne-ver know just how much— I miss you,———

you'll ne ver know just how much— I care.———

And if I tried,— I still could-n't hide— my love for you,

You said good- bye,— now stars in the sky— re - fuse to shine,

SWINGING ON A STAR

Words by JOHNNY BURKE
Music by JIMMY VAN HEUSEN

Would you like to swing on a star, car-ry moon-beams home in a jar,_____ and be bet-ter off than you are, or would you ra-ther be a mule?_____

A mule is an a-ni-mal with
pig is an a-ni-mal with
fish won't do a-ny-thing but

YOU MAKE ME FEEL SO YOUNG

Words by MACK GORDON
Music by JOSEF JOE MYROW

Moderately, with a lilt

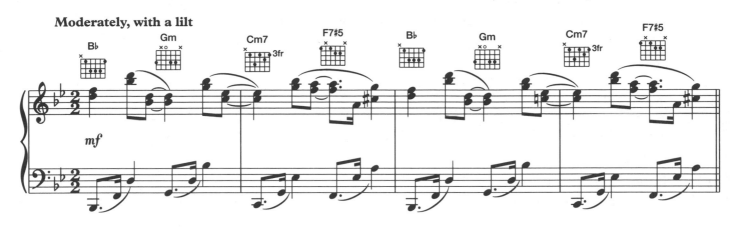

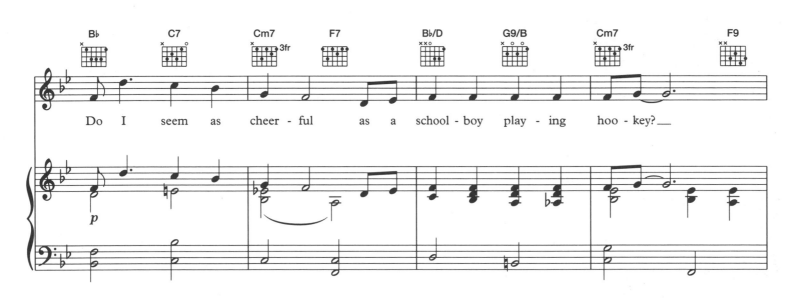

Do I seem as cheer-ful as a school-boy play-ing hoo-key?

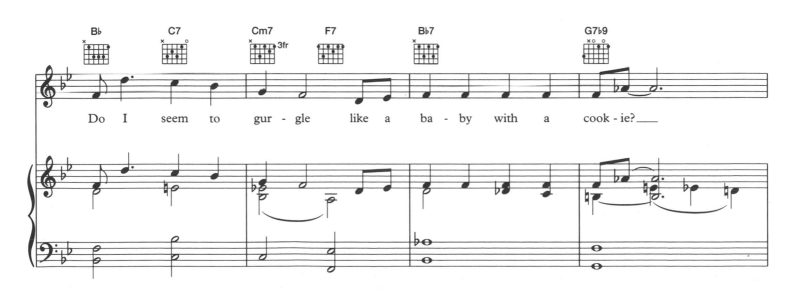

Do I seem to gur-gle like a ba-by with a cook-ie?

BEYOND THE SEA (LA MER)

Original Words and Music by
CHARLES TRENET and ALBERT LASRY
English Words by JACK LAWRENCE

ALMOST LIKE BEING IN LOVE

Words by ALAN JAY LERNER
Music by FREDERICK LOEWE

NATURE BOY

Words and Music by EDEN AHBEZ

CHERRY PINK AND APPLE BLOSSOM WHITE

Words by MACK DAVID
Music by LOUIGUY

say.　　　　The sto - ry goes that once a - go.　　　The boy looked

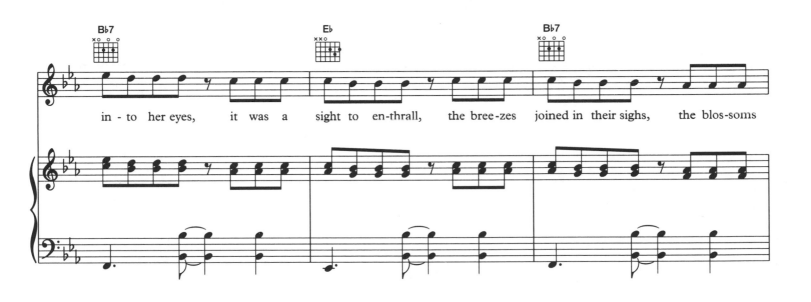

in - to her eyes,　it was a　sight to en-thrall,　the bree-zes　joined in their sighs,　the blos-soms

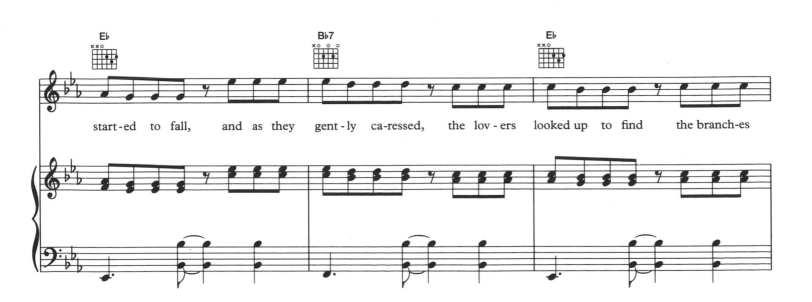

start-ed to fall,　and as they gent-ly ca-ressed,　the lov-ers　looked up to find　the branch-es

of the two trees were in - ter - twined, and that is why the po - ets al - ways write,

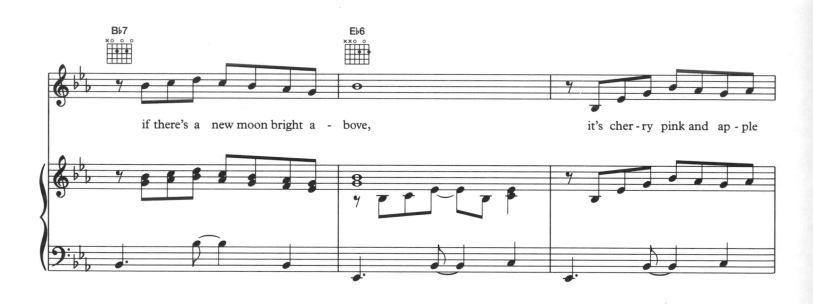

if there's a new moon bright a - bove, it's cher - ry pink and ap - ple

blos - som white when you're in love.

MONA LISA

Words and Music by
JAY LIVINGSTON and RAY EVANS

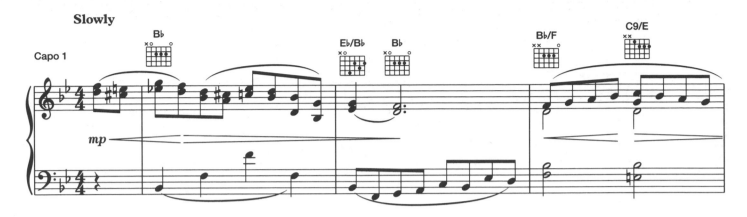

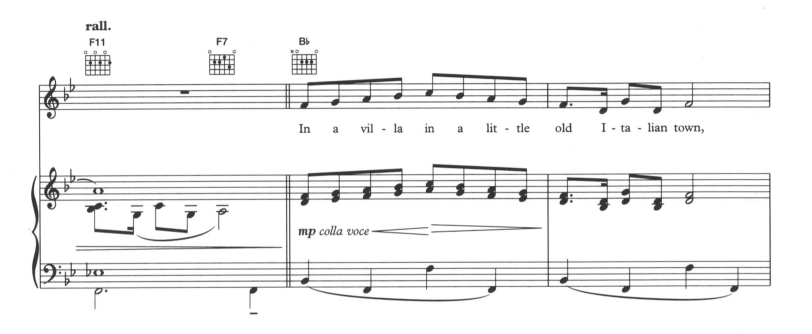

In a vil - la in a lit - tle old I - ta - lian town,

lives a girl whose beau - ty shames the rose. Ma - ny yearn to love her, but their

BLUE VELVET

Words and Music by
BERNIE WAYNE and LEE MORRIS

WHEN I FALL IN LOVE

Words by EDWARD HEYMAN
Music by VICTOR YOUNG

ROCK AROUND THE CLOCK

Words and Music by
MAX C FREEDMAN and JIMMY DAKNIGHT

Moderato

One, two, three 'o-clock, four 'o-clock, rock, five, six, sev-en 'o-clock,

eight 'o-clock, rock, nine, ten e-lev-en 'o-clock, twelve 'o-clock rock, we're gon-na

rock a - round the clock to night.___

1. Put your glad rags on and
(2.) clock strikes two, and
(3.) chimes ring five and
(4.) eight, nine, ten, e -
(5.) clock strikes twelve, we'll

join me, hon,___ We'll have some fun when the clock strikes one,___ we're gon - na
three and four,___ if the band slows down we'll yell for more,
six and seven,___ we'll be rock - in' up in sev - enth heav'n,
lev - en, too,___ I'll be go - in' strong and so will you,
cool off, then,___ start a rock - in' 'round the clock a - gain,

rock a - round the clock to - night,___ we're gon - na rock, rock, rock, 'til

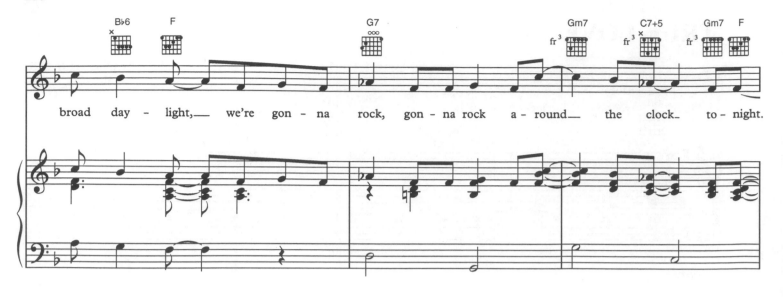

broad day – light,___ we're gon – na rock, gon – na rock a – round___ the clock___ to – night.

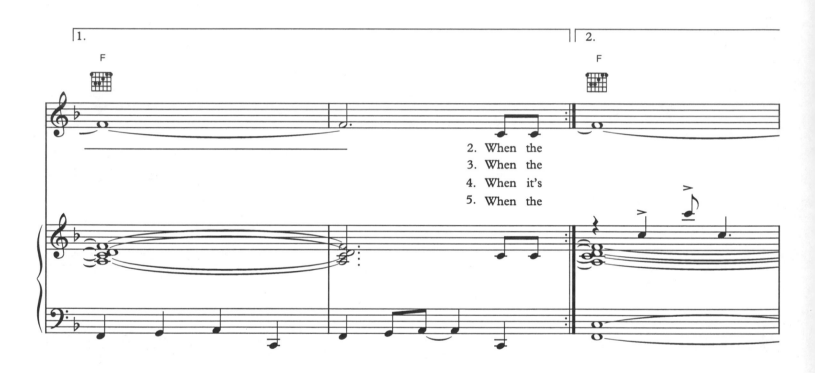

2. When the
3. When the
4. When it's
5. When the

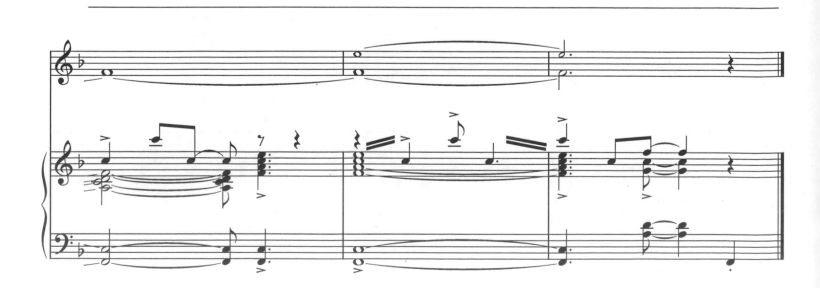

TRUE LOVE

Words and Music by COLE PORTER

EARTH ANGEL (WILL YOU BE MINE)

Words and Music by
CURTIS EDWARD WILLIAMS,
GAYNEL HODGE and JESSE L BELVIN

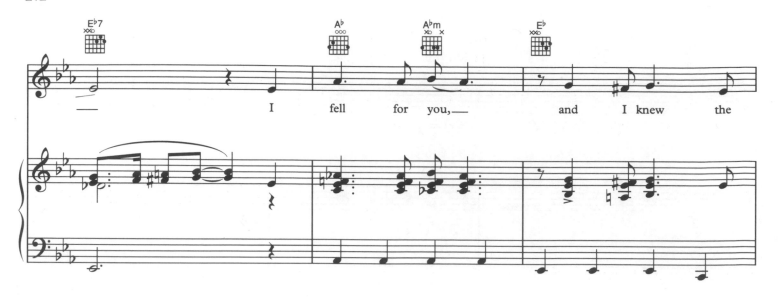

I fell for you,___ and I knew the

vi‑sion of your love's love‑li‑ness,___ I hope and I pray___

that some day___ I'll be the vi‑sion of your hap‑pi‑ness. Earth

FEVER

Words and Music by
JOHN DAVENPORT and EDDIE COOLEY

1. Nev-er know how much I love you, Nev-er know how much I
2. Sun lights up the day-time, Moon lights up the

care.
night.

When you put your arms a-round me, I get a
I light up when you call my name, And you

fe-ver that's so hard to bear.
know I'm gon-na treat you right.
You give me fe-ver

Verse 3 Romeo loved Juliet
Juliet she felt the same,
When he put his arms around her, he said,
"Julie, baby you're my flame."

Chorus Thou givest fever, when we kisset'
Fever with my flaming youth,
Fever – I'm afire
Fever, yea I burn forsooth.

Verse 4 Captain Smith and Pocahantas
Had a very mad affair,
When her Daddy tried to kill him, she said,
"Daddy-o don't you dare."

Chorus Give me fever, with his kisses,
Fever when he holds me tight.
Fever – I'm his Missus
Oh Daddy won't you treat him right.

Verse 5 Now you've listened to my story
Here's the point that I have made:
Chicks were born to give you fever
Be it fahrenheit or centigrade.

Chorus They give you fever when you kiss them,
Fever if you live and learn.
Fever – till you sizzle
What a lovely way to burn.

OH! CAROL

Words and Music by
NEIL SEDAKA and HOWARD GREENFIELD

GREAT BALLS OF FIRE

Words and Music by
JACK HAMMER and OTIS BLACKWELL

Bright rock tempo

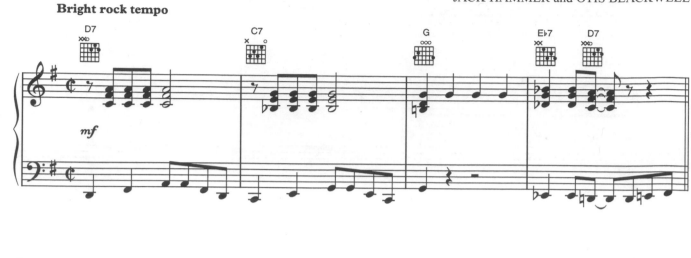

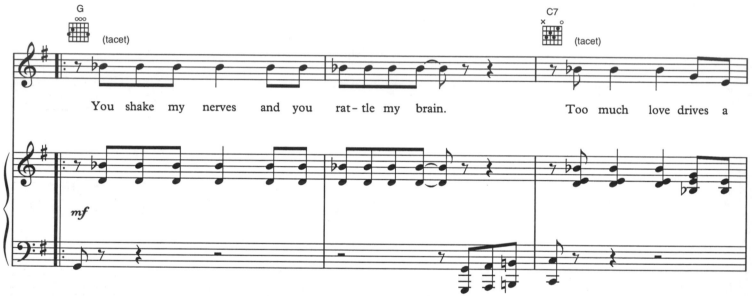

You shake my nerves and you rat‑tle my brain. Too much love drives a

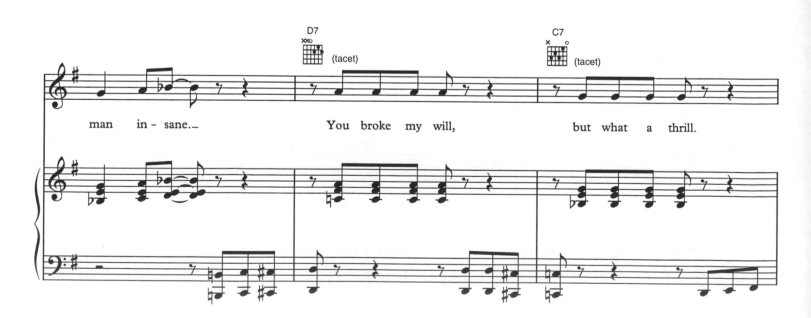

man in‑sane.＿ You broke my will, but what a thrill.

Good - ness gra - cious, Great___ Balls of Fi - re! I laughed at love 'cause I

thought it was fun - ny. You came a - long and moved___ me, hon - ey.

I changed my mind, this love is fine. Good - ness gra - cious, Great

Balls of Fi - re! Kiss me, ba - by, Oh, yo! It feels

good. Hold, me, ba - by. I want to love you like a

lov - er should. You're fine,___ so kind.___ I'm

DREAM LOVER

Words and Music by BOBBY DARIN

CAN'T HELP FALLING IN LOVE

Words and Music by GEORGE WEISS,
HUGO PERETTI and LUIGI CREATORE

THREE STEPS TO HEAVEN

Words and Music by
BOB COCHRAN and EDDIE COCHRAN

THE FIRST TIME EVER I SAW YOUR FACE

Words and Music by EWAN MacCOLL

The first time ____ ev-er I saw your face, ____

I thought the sun ____ rose ____ in your eyes ____

2. The first time ever I kissed your mouth
   I felt the earth move in my hand,
   Like the trembling heart of a captive bird
   That was there at my command, my love,
   That was there at my command.

3. The first time ever I lay with you
   And felt your heart so close to mine,
   And I knew our joy would fill the earth
   And last till the end of time, my love.
   The first time ever I saw your face,
   Your face, your face, your face.

CLOSE TO YOU (THEY LONG TO BE)

Words by HAL DAVID
Music by BURT BACHARACH

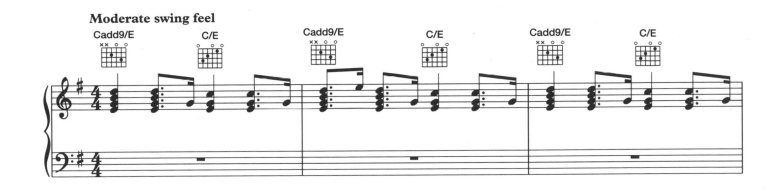

1. Why do birds sud-den-ly ap-pear ev-ery
(2.) why all the boys in town fol-low

time you are near,
you all a-round, just like me___ they long to be

I GET AROUND

Words and Music by BRIAN WILSON

A GROOVY KIND OF LOVE

Words and Music by
TONI WINE and CAROLE BAYER-SAGER

Moderately

When I'm feel-in'

blue, all I have to do is take a look at you, then I'm not so

blue, when you're close to me, I can feel your heart beat, I can hear you

GOOD VIBRATIONS

Words and Music by
BRIAN WILSON and MIKE LOVE

(SITTIN' ON) THE DOCK OF THE BAY

Words and Music by
OTIS REDDING and STEVE CROPPER

Sit-tin' in the morn-ing sun,___ I'll be sit-tin' 'til the eve-nin'___ come,
Left my home in Geor-gia, head-ed for the Fris-co___ Bay.___
Sit-tin' here rest-in' my bones___ and this lone-li-ness won't leave me a-lone.

— watch-in' the ships roll in,___ then I
— I have no-thing to live___ for, look like
— Two thou-sand miles I roam___ just to

WHERE DO YOU GO TO MY LOVELY

Words and Music by PETER SARSTEDT

3 I've seen all your qualifications
   You got from Sorbonne
   And the painting you stole from Piccasso
   Your loveliness goes on and on, yes it does

4 When you go on your summer vacation
   You go to Juan le Pain
   With your carefully designed topless swimsuit
   You get an even suntan, on your back and on your legs

5 And when the snow falls you're found in St. Moritz
   With the others of the Jet-Set
   And you sip your Napoleon brandy
   But you never get your lips wet, no you don't

6 Your name it is heard in high places
   You know the Aga Kahn
   He sent you a race horse for Christmas
   And You keep it just for fun, for a laugh, ha ha ha

7 They say that when you get married
   It'll be to a millionaire
   But they don't realise where you came from
   And I wonder if they really care, or give a damn

8 I remember the back streets of Naples
   Two children begging in rags
   Both touched with a burning ambition
   To shake off their lowly born tags, they try

9 So look into my face Marie-Claire
   And remember just who you are
   Then go and forget me forever
   But I know you still bear the scar, deep inside, yes you do

WE HAVE ALL THE TIME IN THE WORLD

Words by HAL DAVID
Music by JOHN BARRY

MOONDANCE

Words and Music by VAN MORRISON

1. Well it's a mar-vel-lous night for a moon-dance, with the
(Verse 2 see block lyric; Verses 3-7 ad lib. instrumental)

3.

Gm7   C   N.C.   Cm

Can   I   just have   one   more   moon - dance   with   you,

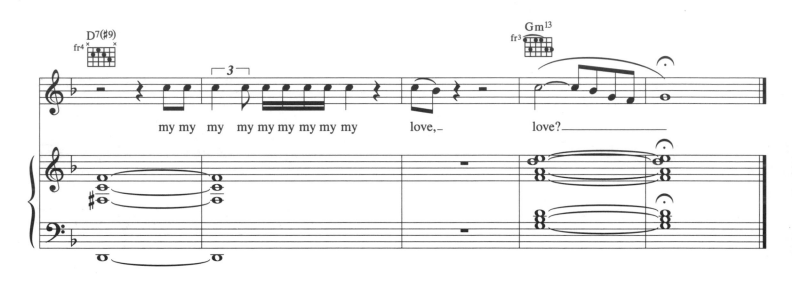

D7(#9)   Gm13

my my   my   my my my my my my   love,   love?

Verse 2:
Well I wanna make love to you tonight,
I can't wait till the morning has come.
And I know now the timing is just right,
And straight into my arms you will run.
And when you come my heart will be waiting
To make sure that you're never alone.
There and then all my dreams will come true dear;
There and then I will make you my own.
Every time I touch you, you just tremble inside.
And I know how much I want you baby,
That you can't hide.
Can I just have one more moondance with you, my love?
Can I just make some more romance with you, my love?

DON'T LET THE SUN GO DOWN ON ME

Words and Music by
ELTON JOHN and BERNIE TAUPIN

YOU'VE GOT A FRIEND

Words and Music by CAROLE KING

ME AND MRS JONES

Words and Music by LEON HURR,
KENNETH GAMBLE and CARY GILBERT

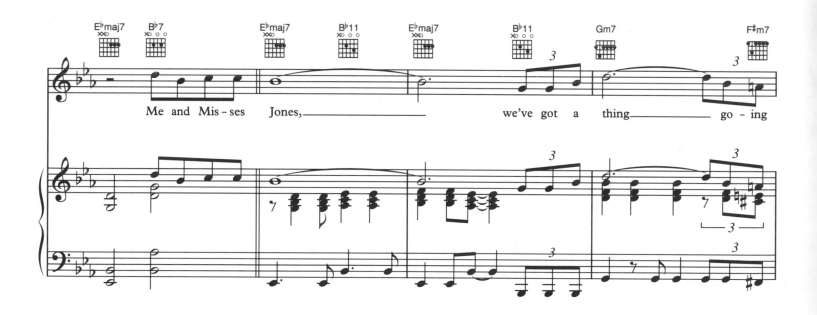

Me and Mis-ses Jones, _____ we've got a thing _____ go-ing

on. We both know that it's wrong,

TOP OF THE WORLD

Words by JOHN BETTIS
Music by RICHARD CARPENTER

Such a feel-ing's com-ing ov-er me. There is
Some-thing in the wind has learned my name and it's

I WILL ALWAYS LOVE YOU

Words and Music by DOLLY PARTON

Verse 3: Instrumental solo

Verse 4:
I hope life treats you kind
And I hope you have all you've dreamed of.
And I wish to you, joy and happiness.
But above all this, I wish you love.
(To Chorus:)

DANCING QUEEN

Words and Music by BENNY ANDERSSON,
STIG ANDERSON and BJÖRN ULVAEUS

Lyrics:

You can dance, you can jive___ hav-ing__ the time of__ your life.___ Oh,___

see that__ girl,__ watch that__ scene__ dig in the danc-ing__ queen.

danc - ing— queen.

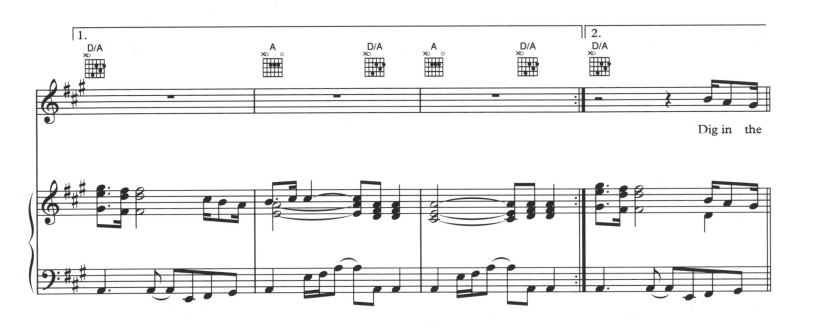

Dig in the

danc - ing— queen.————

repeat and fade

Dig in the

EASY

Words and Music by LIONEL RICHIE

Y.M.C.A.

Words and Music by JACQUES MORALIL,
HENRI BELOLO and VICTOR EDWARD WILLIS

BRIGHT EYES

Words and Music by MIKE BATT

KIDS IN AMERICA

Moderately

Capo 1   N.C.

Words and Music by
MARTY WILDE and RICKY WILDE

Look - ing out a dirt - y old win - dow,
Bright light, the mus - ic gets fast - er,

down be - low the cars in the ci - ty go rush - ing by.
look boy, don't check on your watch, not an - oth - er glance.

I sit here a - lone and I
I'm not leav - ing now, hon - ey,

FAME

Words by DEAN PITCHFORD
Music by MICHAEL GORE

Ba - by, look at me and tell me what you see.
Ba - by, hold me tight, 'cause you can make it right.

1999

Words and Music by PRINCE

I was dream-in' when I wrote this; for-give me if it goes a-stray,
(see additional lyrics)

but when I woke up this morn-ing, could-'ve

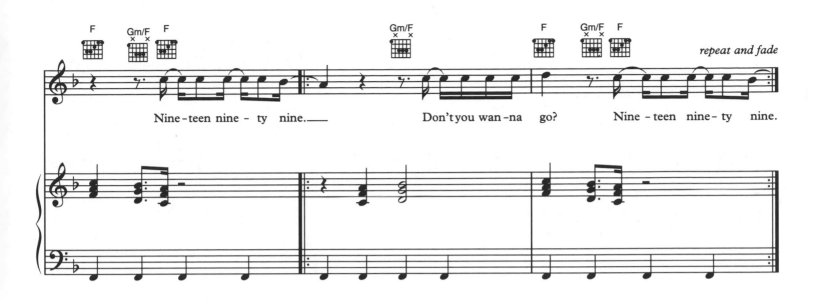

repeat and fade

Nine-teen nine - ty nine._____ Don't you wan -na go? Nine - teen nine - ty nine.

Verse 2:
I was dreamin' when I wrote this
So sue me if I go too fast
But life is just a party
And parties weren't meant to last
War is all around us
My mind says prepare to fight
So if I gotta die I'm gonna
Listen to my body tonight

Verse 3:
If you didn't come to party
Don't bother knockin' on the door
I've got a lion in my pocket
And, baby, he's ready to roar
Everybody's got a bomb
We could all die any day
But before I'll let that happen
I'll dance my life away

TOTAL ECLIPSE OF THE HEART

Words and Music by JIM STEINMAN

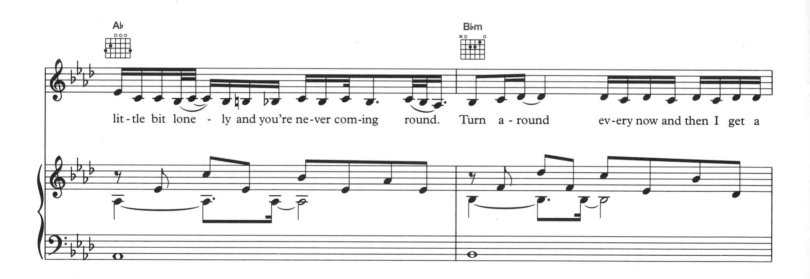

CARELESS WHISPER

Words and Music by
GEORGE MICHAEL and ANDREW RIDGELEY

1. I feel so un - sure as I
2. Time can ne - ver mend the
3. (To) - night the music seems so loud, I wish that we could lose this crowd,

take your hand and lead you to the dance floor;
care - less whis - per of a good friend;
may - be it's bet - ter this way, if we'd hurt each oth - er with the things we want to say. We

THE POWER OF LOVE

Words by JENNIFER RUSH and
MARY SUSAN APPLEGATE
Music by CANDY DE ROUGE and GUNTHER MENDE

The whis-pers__ in the morn-ing__ of lov-ers sleep-ing tight,

are roll-ing by loke thun-der now as I look in your eyes.

I hold on to your bo-dy,__ and feel each move you

times,_____ it seems I'm far a-

NOTHING COMPARES 2 U

Moderately

Words and Music by PRINCE

It's been se-ven hours and fif-teen days since you took your love a-way.

I go out ev-ery night and sleep all day,— since you took your love a-way.

Since you been gone I can do what-ev-er I want,_____ I can see whom-ev-er I choose.

girl, you'd bet-ter try to have fun, no mat-ter what you do. But he's a fool, 'cause

no - thing com-pares, no-thing com-pares 2 U.

No‑thing com‑pares, no‑thing com‑pares 2 U. No‑thing com‑pares,

no‑thing com‑pares 2 U. No‑thing com‑pares,___

no‑thing com‑pares 2 U.

repeat and fade

ANYTHING FOR YOU

Words and Music by GLORIA ESTEFAN

care, and ne-ver leave you. But if that some-one ev - er hurts you, you just might need a friend to turn to.

And I'd do a - ny-thing for you;__ I'll give you up,_____ if

that's what I__ should do_____ to make you hap-py. I can pre - tend each time I see__ you that I don't

care and I____ don't need you. And though in - side I feel__ like dy - ing, you know you'll

GET HERE

Words and Music by BRENDA RUSSELL

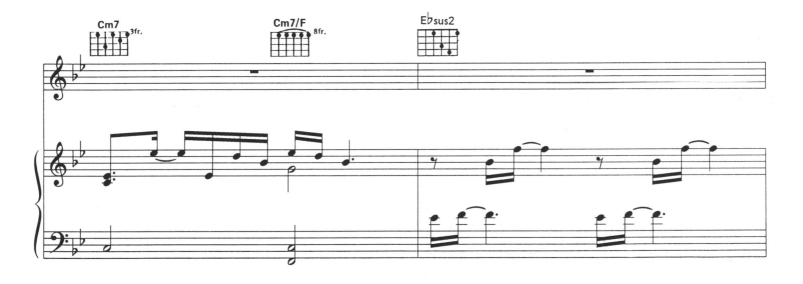

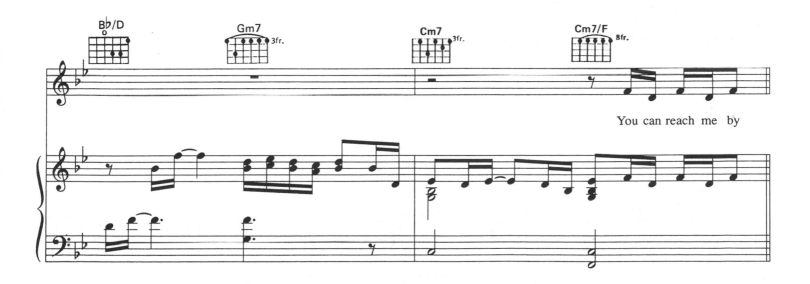

You can reach me by

THE LADY IN RED

Words and Music by CHRIS DE BURGH

It's where I wan-na be.___ But I hard-ly know___

this beau-ty by___ my side,___ I'll ne-ver for-get___

1.
the way you look to-night.___

2.
the way you look___ to-night.___

I will ne-ver—for-get the way you look to-night.—

The la-dy in red.—— My la-dy in red. (I love you)

play 3 times

Verse 2:
I've never seen you looking so gorgeous as you did tonight
I've never seen you shine so bright
You were amazing
I've never seen so many people want to be there by your side
And when you turned to me and smiled
It took my breath away
I have never had such a feeling
Such a feeling of complete and utter love
As I do tonight

MORE THAN WORDS

Words and Music by
NUNO BETTENCOURT and GARY CHERONE

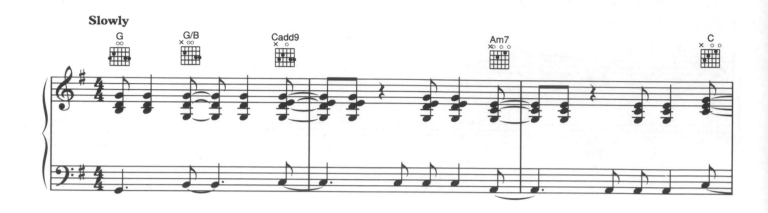

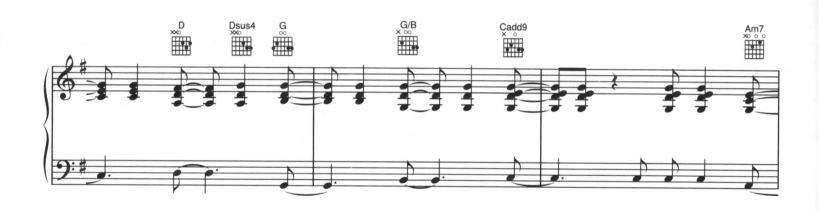

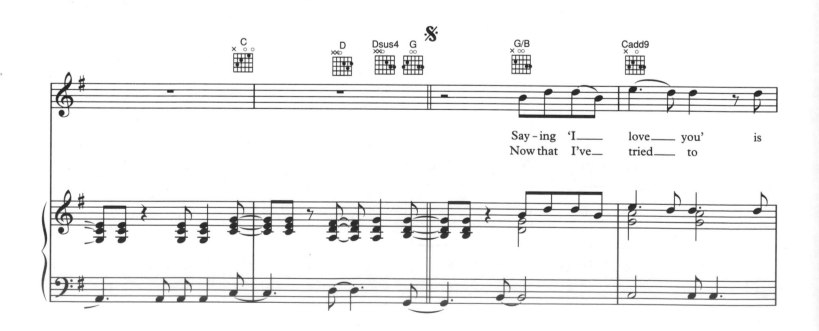

Say - ing 'I___ love___ you' is
Now that I've___ tried___ to

THE SHOOP SHOOP SONG (IT'S IN HIS KISS)

Words and Music by RUDY CLARK

349

A MILLION LOVE SONGS

Words and Music by GARY BARLOW

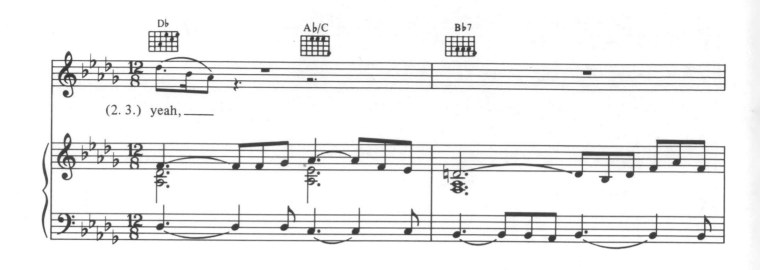

(2. 3.) yeah, ____

Oh

(1.) Put your head a-gainst my life   what do you hear?__   A
(2.) *(See lyric at bottom)*

353

VERSE 2:
Looking to the future now, this is what I see,
A million chances pass me by, a million chances to hold you.
Take me back, take me back to where I used to be,
Hide away from all my truths, through the light I see.

CHORUS:
A million love songs later,
Here I am trying to tell you that I care.
A million love songs later,
And here I am, just for you girl;
A million love songs later,
Here I am.

ALL I WANNA DO

Words and Music by SHERYL CROW,
WILLIAM BOTTRELL, KEVIN GILBERT,
WYN COOPER and DAVID BAERWALD

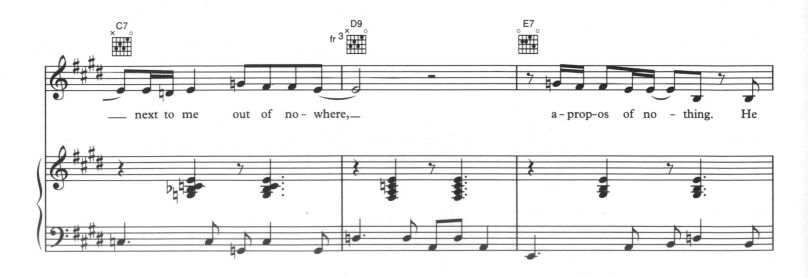

says his name is Wil-liam, but I'm sure he's Bill   or Bil-ly or Mac or Bud-dy.   But he's

plain ug-ly to me   and I won-der if he's ev-er had___ a day of fun in his___whole   life.
(see additional lyrics)

___   We are drink-ing beer at noon on Tues-day   in a   bar___that fac - es a gi-ant

car-wash.   And the good peo-ple of the world are wash-ing their cars on their lunch break,

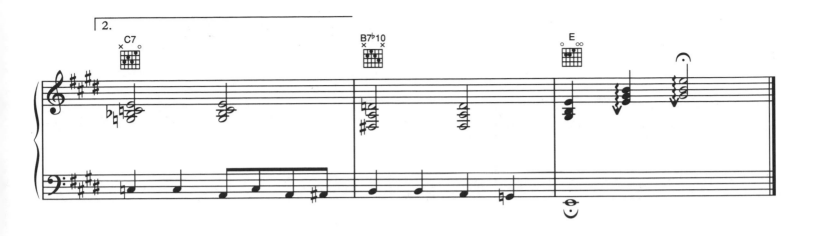

Verse 3:
I like a good beer buzz early in the morning
And Billy likes to peel the labels from his bottles of Bud
And shred them on the bar
Then he lights every match in an oversized pack
Letting each one burn down to his thick fingers
Before blowing and cursing them out
And he's watching the Buds as they spin on the floor
A happy couple enters the bar, dancing dangerously close to one another
The bartender looks up from his want ads

361

JESUS TO A CHILD

Words and Music by GEORGE MICHAEL

Kind-
Sad -

I WANNA BE THE ONLY ONE

Words and Music by
RHETT LAWRENCE and BEBE WINANS

repeat and fade

DON'T SPEAK

Words and Music by
ERIC STEFANI and GWEN STEFANI

It's all end-ing,__ I got-ta stop pre-tend-ing who we are.__

You and me

I can see us dy - ing. Are____ we?____

MY HEART WILL GO ON

Words by WILL JENNINGS
Music by JAMES HORNER

WHEN YOU SAY NOTHING AT ALL

Words and Music by
PAUL OVERSTREET and DON SCHLITZ

1. It's a-maz-ing how you can speak right— to my heart,
(Verse 2 see block lyric)

with-out say-ing a word

you can light up the dark.

Try as I may I can nev-er ex-plain___ what I hear___ when you don't___

___ say a thing.___ The

smile on your face lets me know___ that you need___ me. There's a

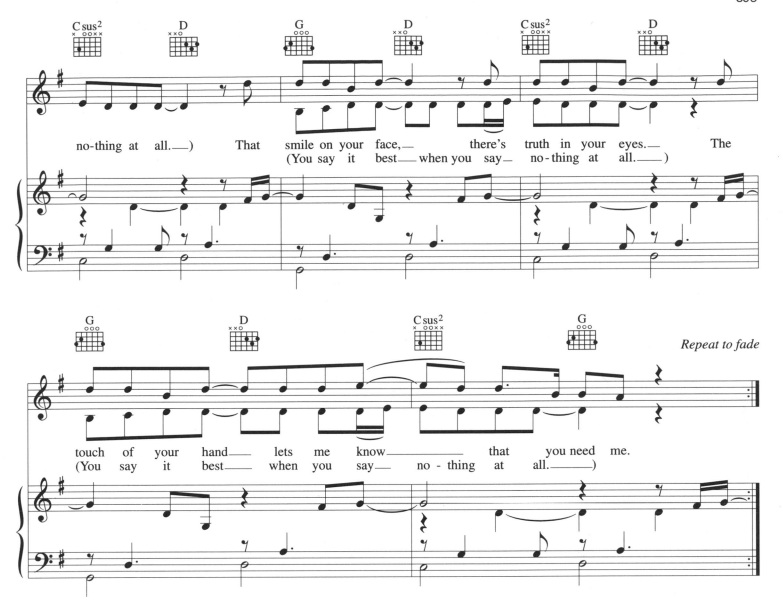

no-thing at all.—) That smile on your face,— there's truth in your eyes.— The
(You say it best— when you say— no-thing at all.—)

touch of your hand— lets me know— that you need me.
(You say it best— when you say— no - thing at all.—)

Repeat to fade

Verse 2:
All day long I can hear people talking out loud
But when you hold me you drown out the crowd
Try as they may they can never defy
What's been said between your heart and mine.

The smile on your face *etc.*

ANGELS

Words and Music by
ROBBIE WILLIAMS and GUY CHAMBERS